ROADS & TRAILS OF NORTH WALES

Tim Prevett

DEDICATION

To my Mother and Father:

Thank you.

Photo Credits

Sychnant Pass and Horseshoe Pass Postcards pre-1925 used with permission (©) Judges of Hastings, 01424 420919, www.judges.co.uk.

Pont Pen-y-benglog, Llanberis Pass and Aberglasyln Pass Postcards pre-1925. No attributable publisher or copyright holder identifiable. Information pertaining to likely copyright holder welcome.

Roman Milestone picture taken at, and used with kind permission of Segontium Museum, Caernarfon, www.segontium.org.uk.

Prehistoric Tools picture taken by arrangement and kind permission from Borough Museum and Art Gallery, Newcastle-under-Lyme.

Photos of Roman Road Stratigraphy and Tethering Stone at Chester Amphitheatre taken by the author on excavation open days, courtesy of Chester City Council and English Heritage.

Photo approaching Penmaenmawr Headland by Helen Prevett.

All other photographs taken by the author.

Every effort has been made to obtain permission from landowners where relevant and identifiable, and to be non-intrusive where private roadside dwellings (such as toll houses) are concerned.

Anyone identifiable in the pictures has consented to their image being used.

Acknowledgements

The assistance of several people (principally in terms of providing lifts and company over many years before I learned to drive) ought to be noted. Over the years I had lifts from Barry Teague, Eileen Roche, Jezreell, Alan Bowers and Cassie, Glenn O'Raw, John Emerich and Alastair McIvor, through various parts of North Wales. Should anyone have been omitted from this list, my gratitude extends to you too.

Thanks to Cerridwen Connelly for supplying and allowing replication of her notes on Welsh pronunciation from her Welsh course, which form Appendix 1.

Appreciation to Andy Norfolk for material concerning Sarn Elen, and to Janet Bord for information and discussion about pilgrim roads and holy wells.

Gratitude to Andy Burnham and the team at the Megalithic Portal for ongoing support and encouragement in all things ancient, from prehistory to holy wells and 'Dark Age' monuments.

To all the drivers who have been stuck behind me along a number of these roads as I observed the road and landscape with care: thank you.

Gwynedd Archaeological Trust in Bangor, in particular Nina Steele and David Hopewell.

Clwyd Powys Archaeological Trust in Welshpool, in particular Jeff Spencer and Charlotte Baxter.

ROADS & TRACKWAYS
OF NORTH WALES

Tim Prevett

Landmark Publishing

Published by

Landmark Publishing

The Oaks, Moor Farm Road West, Ashbourne, DE6 1HD
Tel: (01335) 347349 Fax: (01335) 347303
Email: landmark@clara.net Web: www.landmarkpublishing.co.uk

1st Edition
ISBN: 1 978-1-84306-420-6

Printed by: TJ Internatiional, Cornwall
Design & Cartography: Michelle Prost
Edited by: Louise Maskill

Front cover: The old drovers road to Rowen from Abergwyngregyn
Back cover Top: The modern minor road a short distance north-west of Sarn
Elen from Tomen Y Mur, before it intersects the B4391
Back Cover Bottom Left: The churchyard at St Tanwg's near Harlech
Back Cover Bottom Right: Pont Pen-y-benglog between the Ogwen Valley and Nant Ffrancon
Page 3: The Pass of Llanberis at Pont y Gromlech

Contents

Preface

Love them or hate them, roads have always been a necessary part of human existence and will remain so for as long as our species exists upon the planet. Where there is humanity, there is a need to sell, buy, move and have physical lines of communication in order to survive and to maintain and improve quality of life. The more humans living, the greater and more necessary those routes will be. The empire of the roads nowadays dominates natural landscapes, residential areas and industrial sites. All have been or are being redefined as a result.

It seems everything must bow to the imperative of enabling the engorgement of routes with more vehicles for more journeys. Once the routes were there to serve the communities and industries that were linked by them. Now life and industry need to orient themselves according to the roads.

The growth of population and the advent of new technologies go hand in hand with the improvement of routes that may be millennia old. Likewise the ability to construct new ways where previously there were none facilitates the opening up of remote areas in a way which would once have been thought impossible. Even so, the challenges of geography, topography and climate continue to dictate the routes mortals can take upon the relatively immortal landscape.

A forceful illustration of this occurred in the early part of bringing this book together. A trip to Anglesey was diverted on the return route, where a rockfall onto the A55 had closed the road. The tunnel at Penmaenbach through a mountainous headland jutting into the sea makes the North Wales coastal drive much simpler than it had been before. Even so, the mountain spoke, and the traffic stopped. The flow was redirected to Betws y Coed, diverting traffic away from the modern route which technology had sent under the Conwy estuary and through a mountain. Some tiny fragments of the land thwarted human effort, albeit for a few hours. Therein lies a reminder.

Remove modern technology, which enabled much shorter and better-surfaced routes to be constructed, and the act of travel through the North Wales landscape which can be traversed so easily with little thought and effort becomes a huge endeavour, not for the faint-hearted.

One can drive from Chester to Holyhead within two hours, subject to traffic and roadworks. Speaking of the 'coastal highway' between Conway and Bangor, "The A55 is straight… and fast, so you may not have noticed the hamlet of Aber that the road sweeps by". (1) Even the routes away from the coast lend themselves to speed. Driving many of these routes to observe the roads and landscape, even at the speed limit, gave many instances of impatient drivers wanting to pass with no thought for the history and the landscape around them that have dictated the route they are forced to take.

Following Telford's A5 route and the earlier coach road, one is greeted by a succession of signs flagging up that this is an "Historic Route". This ignores the fact that there are many other historic routes etched in the North Wales valleys, mountains and pastures which are ten, even twenty or more times older than this relative infant of a road placed here in the nineteenth century.

The nomadic travellers of Paleolithic and Mesolithic prehistory, the increased domestication of animals and the farming revolution of the Neolithic period six thousand years ago, through to ritual monuments, defended settlements of Iron Age hill forts, invasion and conquest, huge movements of livestock to feed population centres, and political unions of countries – all have forced into the land a memory of their passing. Consequently the danger in authoring this book has lain in making it into a history of every major human development and event within the given landscape. While the book's focus is on the routes, other details are included where they are expressly relevant and necessary to the intent.

The first chapter details the key developments that have impacted the growth of roads and trackways in North Wales. The remainder of the chapters go into greater detail tracing many of those routes. The geographical coverage extends as far south as Welshpool and Berriew, westwards to Mallwyd, Dinas Mawddy, and the north side of the Mawddach estuary to Barmouth. From that southerly limit the coverage reaches northwards – to the coastline from the Dee estuary in the east, to Anglesey, and Bardsey Island off the Lleyn Peninsula in the west. The border with England to the east is occasionally crossed where pertinent to a given route's origin or destination.

Recognising that many routes are multiperiod, or that earlier traces of roads may now be nowhere to be seen, the greater emphasis will be given to the most enduring or well known part of a route.

The geographical and historical scope of this work is extensive, but it cannot claim to be exhaustive. A comprehensive overview of historical periods and routes is intended, with leads from the bibliography for in-depth follow-up. There will have been oversights and omissions. Corrections and new information are welcome, and the work's selectivity is recognised.

Some may feel a work such as this ought to address ley lines (whether in terms of the physical alignments of Alfred Watkins' "Old Straight Track", or the modern concept of such lines as part of lines of power and geopathic stress etc.). There are other metaphysical explorations of landscapes relating to consciousness, paths of the dead and geopsychology. While such subjects are tangentially related, and make for engaging areas of research in their own right, they are not within the remit of this particular work.

The routes to be covered are predominantly through-routes, with one exception from the prehistoric period. To that end, the surviving remains of tracks relating to industries such as peat cutting or slate extraction are not covered. Similarly, routes relating to localised livestock movements are not included.

This is not a walking guide. It is, however, intended as a usable work, to be employed in concert with maps as a catalyst for exploring and understanding the landscape and routes defined by the landscape – what is today termed the 'Historic Environment'. Other volumes have sought to deal with particular types of tracks with extensive diversions and instructions on walking the wider landscape. To maintain focus, detailed localised walks that incorporate parts of ancient routes on a piecemeal basis are not included in this work. Individual sites or locations which are not part of a route, but which serve by way of useful illustration, are.

Concerning sources: information on Roman roads has been drawn from many cross references discovered whilst researching prehistoric monuments, including Waddelove's unique investigative work about North Wales, and the Roman Roads reports carried out by Gwynedd Archaeological Trust and Clwyd Powys Archaeological Trust. (2)

Information concerning drovers' roads from the Lleyn Peninsula through to Harlech has been sourced from Toulson and Godwin's seminal book (3), which contains many walks and wayside departures from the drove routes. Information on the northern routes from Anglesey has been the most difficult to come by; Wright's book documenting the history of the Eisteddfod at Llangollen has been the primary source on these, as it documents Llangollen's role as the converging point for many droves. This has been augmented by searches of the Historic Environment Record database, which for Wales is 'Coflein'. This has given helpful results, aided by some field research, and the occasional fortuitous anecdote as a passing reference in a book or conversation. All research has been supplemented by information boards in museums, or in churches, buildings and at roadsides visited where relevant. If one comes across a town or village information board, do take a look. Many useful clues have been discovered through these.

While acknowledging reliance upon these sources for route information, the book takes a different approach in relating this information. If this work generates further interest in specific routes or periods, the reader is encouraged to obtain the volumes referred to and absorb the authors' more precise interpretations and evidence given through their eyes and minds first-hand. Many worthwhile hours of reading, and even more of exploring the routes in person, will be obtained. Care has been taken to be accurate or at least sensible in the relating of routes. In leaning on other sources, the intention is to faithfully relate their information, but not so closely that the retelling is merely a duplication. If the content of this book succeeds in only one area, it should be that the volume acts as a catalyst to thinking about how humans have interacted with and traversed the landscape, and prompts more people to study these routes, researching, confirming or rebutting as necessary.

This work presents the routes with further inference to prehistoric routes, settlements and markers where there is evidence of activity before the Romans. Having worked as a Roman tour guide in Chester for a number of years, taking thousands of adults and many thousands of school children around the main Roman features of the city, it is clear that the native British before the Romans are 'dumbed down' and glossed over by many syllabuses and even by the media and documentary makers. If only as a necessary prerequisite for the coming of Rome, prehistory is briefly examined. The Boudiccan revolt is the first reference for many as to the way of life native to these shores in the years BC, ignoring four millennia of impressive structures arranged with deliberation and intelligence by our ancestors.

According to the definition of the word 'prehistory', historical studies and explorations fail to take much account of what happened before writing was introduced to the country. Indeed, history is based upon writing and prehistory upon archaeology, but to exclude the latter from the former on the basis of semantic pedantry is injurious to the understanding of the flow of human development and movement. One can get the impression that impressive monuments and dense settlements, and, yes, even roads first arrived with the civilising conquest of Rome. Not so. There were roads and trackways before the Romans constructed their routes or improved native British thoroughfares.

This book seeks to address and suggest the usage of prehistoric monuments as waymarkers for routes, and bring the attention of a wider readership to the intelligence, workmanship and basic infrastructure of the native British. Some clear pre-Roman routes are noted, and where later routes pass by selected prehistoric monuments and settlements, this will be noted too. For the first time, the megalithically dense island of Anglesey is considered in terms of its prehistoric trackways.

To state the obvious – people have always needed to arrive at, live in, interact with and depart from their locale. Excepting dramatic innovations in road-building technology, such as floating prefabricated concrete tunnels across an estuary to form a crossing (as in Conwy), or boring holes through mountainous headlands, or the spirit of innovation in the construction of the Menai Bridge, it is arguable that many routes, especially in more remote or rural areas, could well have remained the same since the last ice age scoured its heavy imprint on the land, forming many of the deep structures of the topography.

Concerning safety for those wanting to explore these routes for themselves: the North Wales landscape is hazardous, the mountains particularly so. Adverse weather conditions at a moment's notice, blanket bogs and precipitous drops are among the hazards to be anticipated. Common sense in conjunction with appropriate clothing, footwear, Ordnance Survey maps (1:25,000 scale) and attention to local knowledge and weather warnings are prerequisite.

Bill Bryson's introduction to North Wales is not very promising: "From the train, north Wales looked like holiday hell – endless ranks of prison-camp caravan parks standing in fields in the middle of a lonely, wind beaten nowhere, on the wrong side of the railway line and a merciless dual carriageway." (4) The routes described herein have been just as merciless in the past, albeit in a way unimaginable to most of today's car-comforted travellers, though they remain infinitely more interesting than the monotony of being held up in traffic jams, or alternatively travelling at 70 miles per hour with no regard for the landscape and the ways in which it has been traversed in the past.

This book has its origins as an affiliated activity with the Time Team Big Roman Dig in July 2004

– though many parts of it weave their threads from before then. From looking at the Roman road from Canovium to Segontium (the forts at Conwy and Caernarfon), the research grew into this work to look at roads and trackways across all periods. The research will continue beyond publication; should the reader wish to join in further discussion, there is a group on the social networking site "Facebook", which can be reached through the address www.roadsandtrackwaysofnorthwales.org.uk. The author can be contacted directly through tim@roadsandtrackwaysofnorthwales.org.uk.

Any mention of modern road-numbering in conjunction with older routes is to place the ancient ways in a frame of reference familiar to users of today's maps and road atlases; no anachronism is meant or implied.

Do enjoy exploring the roads and trackways of North Wales. The intention is that the reader will never see moving in this landscape in the same way again, and will have unlocked for them a land arguably unparalleled in its layering of stunning scenery, history, archaeology, myths, legends, saints and stones – all using and making roads and trackways, most of which are still with us in one form or another today.

List of Maps

CHAPTER 1

Overview of Roads & Trackways of North Wales

The information we now have about travel is unprecedented. Even the 1:25000 maps many use for outdoor activities were unheard of until quite recently. Now we are able to sit at home with up-to-date traffic and weather reports on given routes, with webcams showing the A55 North Wales Express Way flowing (or not). Not so long ago this would have been unthinkable. Using such software as Google Earth to fly through terrain with 3D depictions of the landscape beneath, either side, or mountains towering above is without precedent until the past few years. From the comfort of our living rooms, subject to screen resolution, we can view well-worn tracks and even earthworks of significant historical sites at our leisure.

Then there are the satellite navigation systems that instruct us about which way to go, with allegedly superior knowledge and directions sent from around the globe via orbiting spacecraft. Like any technological brain, they lack several things. 'Satnavs' used without accompanying hard maps, common sense, or local knowledge are not so handy as may at first be expected. For the walker somewhat more in touch with their environment than the comfortably-numbed modern motorist, GPS units are an invaluable aid in ascertaining one's location in barren wilderness, or in finding that landmark or monument. Until the advent of widely accessible cartography, satellite navigation aids, and internet information, things were not so easy.

The traveller had to deal with the challenges of a given route as they happened, hoping for a combination of luck, local knowledge, and favourable weather. The same is true for the travellers of today, albeit with the illusory expectation that a journey across large parts of the landscape should go without incident, problem, or trepidation. Until the last century, developing and using the roads and trackways of North Wales, or indeed anywhere, was something for the determined. Given the effort of those who first wore the routes into the ground, surfaced them, or implemented new road technology (as will be seen), perhaps modern road usage ought to revise the assumed right to an easy journey. Relatively carefree long journeys are a recent development. Perhaps the time will come again when many of the ancient roads and trackways will come into use depending on how the theatre of humanity fares upon the planetary stage.

The Earliest Routes

Movement within a landscape is an existential prerequisite for humans. To hunt, to survive, to live in an appropriate environment subject to the climate, to trade, to communicate – every action, every product necessary for life requires some movement from A to B.

The earliest evidence of human settlement in North Wales is at Bontnewydd (SJ009712) in Denbighshire, north-west from Denbigh, dating from the Lower Palaeolithic (Old Stone Age; owing to its enormous spread over time, the Palaeolithic is divided into Upper, Middle and Lower in terms of chronology). At Bontnewydd, early Neanderthals were living in the limestone cave and hunting in the valleys 225,000 years ago. Given that ice ages came and went with many interglacial periods, the landscape has been extensively rewritten since then. Ridgeways and valley bottoms would have served as principal through-routes before the next known traces of human life came into evidence.

Further evidence of hunter-gatherer activity comes in the form of a leaf-pointed tool from the late Middle Palaeolithic, found at Ffynnon Beuno cave (SJ085725) on the east side of the Vale of Clwyd.

The entrance to Bontnewydd Cave in Denbighshire, containing evidence of the oldest human activity in Wales.

This dates from 36,000 BC, with other tools dating between 28,000 to 26,000 BC – some 200,000 years later than the remains at Bontnewydd. Material from Cae Gwyn cave to the immediate west of Ffynnon Beuno cave also dates from 16,000 BC in the early Upper Palaeolithic.

West of the River Conwy the earliest settlement was at Kendrick's Cave on the Great Orme. Here four human skeletons, a horse jaw-bone decorated with a zigzag pattern, decorated deer teeth, flint implements and likely associated human burial were discovered, dating to an interglacial period around 30,000 BC. As will be seen, the Great Orme continued as a place of significance right up to the Iron Age and beyond, finding a new lease of life with the coming of the trains in the Victorian period by its proximity to Llandudno.

Up to and including the Mesolithic, or Middle Stone Age, transport would have been possible by dugout boats, though these were more suitable for river navigation, not open sea. This would have avoided the need to penetrate the deeply-forested inland areas, although that would have been done where following herds of animals was necessary for supply of meat. An important Mesolithic site in Gwynedd is on the headland near Aberffraw at Trwyn Du (SH352679), where scatterings of flint flakes from the manufacture of points for harpoons, arrows and barbs indicate temporary settlement and movement as the hunter-gatherers continued a largely nomadic existence in search of sustenance. This headland site was reused around 1700 BC in the Bronze Age for a burial cairn, conspicuous upon the landscape as a marker, the kerb stones and small earthworks of which survive

The headland at Trwyn Du near Aberffraw. The only Mesolithic activity in Gwynedd was found at this spot, beneath the later Bronze Age kerb cairn which still marks the location.

to this day near the cliffs.

The Neolithic

Clearance of forests did not begin to happen until the technological revolution of the New Stone Age, or Neolithic, which was characterised by the domestication of animals, the introduction of crop farming, and improved technology in the form of polished axes. Hand axes had been used as tools for hundreds of thousands of years previously, though the types from the Neolithic were more efficient than earlier examples. With increased settlement came the arrival of the megalithic tombs, giving a sense of connection to ancestors gone before, and the inference of lines of communication.

No definite or postulated tracks between monuments of this period survive, though where a Neolithic megalithic tomb survives in proximity to later prehistoric monuments one can reasonably assume ongoing usage of an earlier route.

Megalithic tombs, also known as dolmens (meaning stone table), cromlechs, or tribedd (literally, three graves), come in a variety of styles which are indicative of different types of structures, giving evidence of the movement of ideas, and by inference the movement of peoples. The oldest type of tomb is known as a portal dolmen – typified by an H-shaped arrangement of tall stones, with

A progression of prehistoric tools, from a Palaeolithic Hand Axe (left), Neolithic Axe Heads (centre), a Bronze Age Spearhead (right), and a variety of Mesolithic flints at the bottom. Courtesy of Borough Museum and Art Gallery, Newcastle-under-Lyme.

a high placed slab enclosing a rectangular chamber behind.

From Ireland and the Boyne Valley in particular come the passage graves – mortuary structures for the storage of ancestors' bones, accessed via a passage. Some of these are decorated with rock art, pecked-out incisions giving a variety of patterns – chevrons, lozenges, and abstract shapes. In North Wales these are such places as the earliest part of multiphase Trefignath (SH258806) near Holyhead (the second phase of which infers Scottish contact), Barclodiad-y-Gawres (SH329707), Bryn Celli Ddu (SH507702), Bodwyr (SH462682) and Ty Newydd (SH344738) on Anglesey, with possibly the Gop (SJ086802) in Flintshire. (1) A passage grave exists as far east as Liverpool at the Calder Stones (SJ405875), now situated in a greenhouse in a park of that name, bearing rock art in keeping with examples on Anglesey and in Ireland.

From the Cotswold-Severn area comes a range of tombs characterised by a horn-shaped forecourt area, a type which shows some penetration into what is now Welsh territory. Capel Garmon tomb (SH818543) near Pentrefoelas is a pleasing illustrative restored example of what this would have looked like. An important double site near Harlech is at Dyffryn Ardudwy (SH589228), which has an example of both of the styles of graves – a portal dolmen and a Cotswold-Severn tomb.

It is in the consideration of these tombs that we first meet the significance of Ireland in the development of roads and trackways in North Wales. From these prehistoric links with passage graves in the Boyne Valley, through to the Post Road for Holyhead and Telford's revision and improvement of the London-to-Holyhead ferry road, it is apparent that the links across the Irish Sea have been monumentally influential in affecting traffic through North Wales. Politics, trade, communication and migration have all etched their way into the landscape by their passage in an Irish context, coupled with spiritual quests and conquests at other times. The first area of consideration, though, probably has more of a religious significance – or, as the ubiquitous archaeological phrase goes, "It must be ritual".

Cursus Monuments

The late Neolithic introduces a style of monument that is the first large-scale deliberate adaptation of the land to direct human movement: the cursus monument. Given these are without precedent, and little-known outside specialist interest groups, they are included within this work as part of the evolution of trackways and roads.

Early routes relied upon fortuitous formations of the landscape (i.e. mountain ridges, valley bottoms, passes, and the paths left by animals) and subsequent reuse of those routes to better define them. The cursus is an intentional construction, and the most ancient and only dateable linear earthwork relating to movement. The official definition is given as "a long narrow rectangular earthwork enclosure of Neolithic date, usually defined by a bank and ditch and presumed to be of ceremonial function. Known examples range in length from less than 100m to c.10km." (2)

Cursus monuments are so named because it was originally and misleadingly thought that they were ancient British racecourses – and they were thus ascribed the Latin name for those recreational features. Now they are interpreted as being for ritual use, and a few examples, certain and uncertain, can be found in North Wales. Two definite examples are known – one at Sarn y Bryn Caled, south of Welshpool, which can be seen as an occasional cropmark when conditions are right; and the other on the south-east edge of Bangor, although it is now beneath the Llandegai Industrial Estate. There are other possible cursus monuments within the region, which are examined briefly below.

Another trait of the Neolithic is the hand axes that were quarried from specific volcanic seams in different parts of Britain. Owing to their very specific geological qualities, tracing the origins of these axes is possible, giving a picture of an active industry and the movement of products around the country.

The Bronze Age

The Bronze Age gives rise to further varieties of lithic monuments. Stone circles become more popular, some of which are sited near industrial axe centres, such as the Druids' Circle (SH723746) above Penmaenmawr, or Mitchell's Fold (SO304983) in Shropshire on the very edge of the Welsh border.

Individual standing stones and stone rows were also erected throughout the British Isles during the Bronze Age. Some of these standing stones are spread out through the terrain, forming physical alignments suggesting markers along a route, or sometimes they are in flat valley bottoms where they would be prominent as mileposts of sorts, or indicative of a fording point across a river. Routes such as Llanbedr to Trawsfynydd or Rowen to Bwlch y Ddeufaen are among the most spectacular of the longer alignments, and they are examined in more detail below. Tall menhirs like Aber Rhaedr (SJ138248) near Llanrhaeadr ym Mochnant serve as good examples of valley floor markers.

Large natural glacial erratics – rounded boulders shifted out of their original geological context by the actions of glaciers during ice ages – can also serve as waymarkers, being adopted as standing stones along routes. Examples of these are found again near the Druids' Circle near Penmaenmawr (Maen Crwn at SH731750), and at Bwlch Maen Gwynedd (SJ078336) in the Berwyn Mountains.

More concentrated lines of lithic erections elsewhere in Wales and the British Isles give strong indications of lines of direction and trackways, but North Wales north of the Mawdach estuary has few stone rows of note. A small uncertain alignment on the Great Orme, Hwylfa'r Ceirw (the Path

The Bronze Age trackway running over the Carneddau from the burial monument at Carnedd y Ddelw.

of the Deer) at SH766841 appears to point over a cliff, while three small stones called the Three Leaps at SH528784 on Anglesey are now almost unintelligible in view or purpose. A further two areas of stone rows north of Pentrefoelas adjacent to later drove and mediaeval routes are now overgrown, scattered or toppled out of place, affording little beneficial interpretation to any notion or prescription of passage in the landscape. These are Hafod y Garreg at SH878535, and Hafod y Dre at SH885537. Rhos y Beddau (SJ057301), a certain double stone row in the Berwyn Mountains near Pistyll Rhaeadr, survives well, but is now so remote and low in tall grass in the wilderness that visiting, let alone interpreting it is difficult for all but for the most eager, although it makes for a rewarding visit for the determined enthusiast.

Burial monuments called cairns, consisting of stones piled on top of one another in a circular arrangement, were constructed, sometimes with box-like chambers or 'cists' to inter the deceased in the centre. A related type of monument is the barrow, using soil instead of stones to construct the funerary monument, often with an urn containing cremated remains forming the primary burial within the feature. The word 'cairn' in this work refers solely and exclusively to this sort of construction and not to modern walkers' cairns made as helpful points of reference in often featureless areas and places where a recognisable landmark is needed (though that principle is not without precedent).

Cairns and barrows also have a range of subcategories, but all are monuments of the dead, in contrast to the other lithic monuments of the Bronze Age which were for the living. Often the former are situated upon ridgeways or passes, defining routes so as to inform the traveller about whose territory they are moving in. Good examples of these are on the Carneddau west of the River Conwy; burial monuments are situated upon each of the peaks, Carnedd y Ddelw (SH707706) being the lowest of them with the shortest uphill walk.

A type of feature which indicates movement largely during the Bronze Age (though on occasion the sites do pre- and post-date their principal era) is the burnt mound. In places these sites pepper the wilderness and upland landscapes, and though it is rare they are also found in relatively urban areas, a well known example being in Moseley near Birmingham (SP093820). They are the split remains of rocks used for heating water, discarded in piles after repeated use.

Lacking containers which could survive direct exposure to fire whilst holding water to be heated, people in the Bronze Age constructed a trough – either in rock, or hollowed into a smoother surface and lined with material to help it remain water-tight. A hearth was constructed close by (both trough and hearth being near a ready source of water for obvious reasons). Rocks were heated on the fire, and then removed (one assumes held between two cooler rocks or a very good and early equivalent of quality oven gloves) to place in the water, thereby heating it. The thermal shock of this action would weaken and shatter the rocks, which were subsequently or periodically removed to form a rubbish heap of burnt rocks – i.e. burnt mounds. By this method the water was heated for whatsoever purpose required at the time–, leaving definite evidence of settlement and movement through the landscape.

The Iron Age

In the flow of technological innovation which brought about what is called the Iron Age, society underwent a substantial shift. The transitions between these historical periods did not happen overnight, but filtered in over time. It must be borne in mind that these are our labels for dividing and categorising the past – the ancient British would not have referred to themselves in these terms (or in equivalent language at the time). New technology coupled with environmental disaster were both occurring; if disaster seems too dramatic a term, then certainly climate change and practices which could not yield sustainability of lifestyle for the populace. Humanity has a habit of exhausting its environment, to its own detriment.

In terms of climate, the preceding Bronze Age was much warmer, and with greater settlement populations grew. In places such as the Eglwysegs to the north of Llangollen, this eventually led to over-farming of the upland plateau which supported much activity at the time. With exhausted soils in some places, and the worsening of the climate to colder and wetter weather, the resources to sustain tribal groups were stretched. Around 600 BC society (used as a loose general term) was under great stress, giving rise to the defended hilltop settlements commonly known now as hillforts.

There are no definitive identifiable Iron Age routes surviving, but by extrapolation between the Bronze Age tracks and the coming of the Romans in the middle of the first century AD, it is fair to assume these routes continued in use throughout the Iron Age.

Hearkening back to the influence of the Irish in ancient monuments, there exists a most Hibernian reference to very common Iron Age sites. Look at maps of North Wales for long enough, and the gothic script of "Cytiau'r Gwyddelod" will become apparent in many places. These are the locations of hut circles – the foundations of pre-Roman settlements, often in clusters, and the Welsh name means 'Irishmen's Huts'. A most satisfying example of these is near South Stack on Holy Island on the west side of Anglesey at SH212820. There are many others throughout the region surviving to less spectacular degrees, but all are indicative of belonging to incomers. A similar name occurs at Gwyddelwern on the A494 north-west from Corwen, with the same etymology as the Irishmen's Huts.

On this note the helpfulness of the Welsh language must be articulated. It can help unlock clues as to topography, history, and/or legend. With a litte study, English place names can inform by a similar method, but Welsh, once it is understood somewhat and its pronunciation grappled with, is

The hut circles or Cytiau'r Gwyddelod (Irishmen's Huts) at South Stack, Anglesey.

The Clwydian Range hill fort of Moel y Gaer, with peat cutting marks on the path to Moel Famau; taken on a flight from Exeter to Liverpool.

so much more expressive. This is something which can escape many people, including native speakers. When familiar with a place name, anyone can fail to be cognisant of such a name's significance. George Borrow in his "Wild Wales" relates an interaction with a Welsh woman: "'Is it called Pentre Dwr,' said I, 'because of the water of the brook?' 'Likely enough,' said she, 'but I never thought of the matter before.'" (3)

When presented with the name of a town, church, building, field, lake, waterfall, craggy outcrop on a mountain and so on, examination of those names will more often than not give information of use or interest. Appendices on pronunciation and key words for unlocking the landscape and routes are provided later, and where expressly relevant to the text are included throughout the work.

There were lowland settlements such as homesteads or farmsteads, but the often spectacularly-sited hillforts are the principal obvious monument of the Iron Age. These are typically distributed around coastal regions – sometimes as promontory settlements requiring minimal defensive work. Ramparts and ditches across the neck of land or on one side would give the intended security as opposed to completely circular earthworks. In other locations, forts were clustered on the hilltops above river valleys – giving a supply of water if there were no springs within, or more strategically, allowing supervision of routes through the valleys beneath. The Breidden (SJ292144) between Welshpool and Shrewsbury is a fine example of a fort above vital corridors; further north, the chain of forts from Caer Drewyn (SJ087444) near Corwen in the south to Moel Hiraddug (SJ063785) above Dyserth in the northernmost extreme forms the Clywdian Range, guarding the route of the river Clwyd to the coast, and also the inland route across Flintshire from Chester and England as they now stand. Some forts were constructed of earthen defences with palisades to give additional obstruction on the ramparts, whereas others such as Conwy Mountain hillfort (SH760778) or the diminutive Caer Bach (SH744730) just a little further south had stone topped ramparts. Pen y Gaer (SH750693) fort above the River Conwy has elaborate anti-cavalry and infantry defences known as Chevaux de Frise – rows of angled stones to trip and hinder any charge. Given that elsewhere in Wales these only occur at Castell Henllys in Pembrokeshire, this suggests the continuing movement of people – if not literally in person, then certainly the importation of ideas.

The Roman Conquest

The growing might and attention of the Romans culminated in the invasion of Britain in AD 43 under Claudius' rule. The military machine worked its way north-westwards into what is now Wales, taking nearly 40 years to eventually suppress the British tribes. As noted, "Wales posed something of a problem for the Roman administration: the area was too hostile to be left alone, as it provided a threat to the security of the towns and villas of the peaceful lowlands. It had therefore to be conquered and garrisoned…Even after its final pacification, Wales remained a garrisoned zone…" (4)

The rebel British hero Caratacus (also known as Caradoc), who had resisted the Romans in the south-east of the territory, was handed over in 51AD by the Roman sympathiser Cartimandua. Even with his troublesome example removed, the ancient inhabitants of Wales held out against complete Roman rule for a further quarter of a century.

In 60 AD, Anglesey – the famed hotbed of Druidic learning and antagonistic anti-Roman sentiment – was addressed by the forces of Suetonius Paulinus, gathered on the Menai Strait. The successful slaughter of resistance on Mon Mam Cymru – Anglesey the Mother of Wales – was swiftly followed by a departure back to Chester and the Midlands to see to the Boudiccan revolt which threatened Roman peace and stability –(the Pax Romana) in Britain.

The south of the region, in the Corwen/Bala and Dolgellau areas, held out against the Romans until 77/8 AD under the British tribe known as the Ordovices, but even they succumbed to Roman might, and so the pacification of Wales was achieved. To consolidate the holding of Wales, a chain of forts with supply and communication routes was constructed and garrisoned – a foreshadowing of what would happen again some 1100 or so years later under Edward I.

The Romans brought their particular method of road-making with them; as Edmund Waddelove records: "The most common construction, used over flat or undulating terrain, was the agger, a ridge composed of material excavated from a ditch along the road-line; frequently there was a ditch on both sides and occasionally a third "quarry" ditch … The agger, often referred to as a 'causeway' or a 'ridge', was thoroughly compacted to prevent penetration of the foundation by rainfall and cambered (sloped from the centre to the sides) to shed the water into the ditches. The soil, subsoil and 'parent' natural material were spread across the width of the road in the order in which they were excavated… This… led to clearly distinguishable layers, 'strata', being formed and it is from these words 'street', 'strat', or in Wales 'stryt' or 'stryd'… very often sure indicators of the presence of a Roman road, were derived." (5)

These roads either utilised existing native British routes, or as was typical of Roman road construction, followed the safest, easiest lines to facilitate movement of soldiers, resources and imperial communications. Much of the traffic would have comprised of pack animals and horse-drawn carts and carriages. Mules and oxen would have been among their number.

For the first time the deliberate construction of surfaces to improve the communications infrastructure was brought to Wales. This gave a network of routes throughout the country that were to remain without serious additions or improvements for some 1700 years after their construction. Even with the new road technology, travel through the region remained a major undertaking for another 1400 years after the Roman legions departed.

Showing the stratigraphy of the Roman road at the Chester Amphitheatre Dig where the surface has been repeatedly improved in situ, leading to successive layers of similar material.

Besides milestones, the first historical references to specific routes were picked up in two vital documents: the Antonine Itinerary and the Ravenna Cosmography. The former is traditionally accredited to Antoninus Augustus and commonly dated to the start of the third century AD; it is without equal, being a list of the key stopping-points along the roads of the Roman Empire. For North Wales, the route from Chester (Deva) to Caernarfon (Segontium) is featured as Iter XI, detailing the 74 miles between the two key Roman forts. The Ravenna Cosmography was put together in the seventh century by an unknown person who appeared to have cartographic sources to hand. The document lists places names, and of significance to North Wales are mentions of Chester, Wroxeter, Canovium, Segontium, Forden Gaer (south of Welshpool) and possibly Caer Gai.

Pilgrimage and Spirituality

It is a touch ironic that the land which took four Roman military campaigns to crack later became the refuge for Christianised Romano-British culture. Pagan Germanic peoples came in from the east during the early mediaeval period, leading to Wales becoming a land of Saints and a Christian stronghold.

As previously noted, the Roman routes served North Wales without replacement for centuries, and would have been used in part by those on spiritual or religious missions. An early route based on fifth and sixth century memorial inscriptions is proposed from Llandanwg south of Harlech on an inland way to Chester. Pilgrimage from St David's to Holywell took place on a north-east–south-west route while pilgrims travelled east to west from Chester to Bardsey Island on a more northerly route. There was also a southern approach cutting along the south of the Lleyn Peninsula on the far north-west reach of the Welsh mainland. Other local pilgrimages also took place on lesser scales. The major routes are looked at in Chapter Four.

Early references to passage through the country are found solely in the writings of Giraldus Cambrensis – Gerald of Wales. In 1188 he undertook a 'Journey through Wales' with Archbishop Baldwin to drum up support for a crusade. While an account of the roads and tracks is not the reason for his travelogue (as it would be called today), in places a commentary upon the journey is incidental to their progress. Not much is related concerning North Wales, but where his passage pertains to a particular route some references are given. Further exploration of Giraldus Cambrensis is worthwhile. A shrewd, canny and opinionated character, his writing is full of tales and anecdotes to compete with any noted travel journalist of today.

Some of the earlier routes, in particular the Roman ways, served armies on a further two occasions, but without new tracks or surfaces being made. The conquest of North Wales by King Edward in the late thirteenth century, with his stranglehold and ring of English castles, was enabled by these routes; within another 400 years more armies were on the march along Roman roads as the land was convulsed by Civil War.

Drove Roads and Trackways

Other routes were formed by the sheer numbers of livestock driven through the easiest (and later, cheapest) passage for hundreds of years – the drove roads. The rich agricultural land of the Lleyn Peninsula to the far west and Anglesey to the north-west sustained a wealth of livestock ready to feed the consuming population centres of England, and ultimately, London.

Following the Norman Conquest, growing to its peak in the seventeenth and eighteenth centuries, droving was an epic feature of the Welsh and English (and, of course, the Scottish) countryside, resulting in drove routes. Moore-Colyer gives an in-depth examination of the earlier droves, with some discussion of possible cattle-trading taking place over Offa's Dyke from Wales to England in the late eighth century. The earliest definite date for cattle trade in North Wales is given as 1312, specifically at Ruthin and Abergele in 1347–8, with the first mention of livestock trade from Anglesey in the early fifteenth century. (6)

A number of tracks were widened and used for centuries by these men with their flocks and herds on foot – some of these routes are now main arterial routes, and others have perished or been forgotten in the tracts of wilderness which still persist, impenetrable even to the most hardened and well-equipped of walkers. Closer examination of these routes in particular gives great clarity to understanding just how prohibitive mountains and rivers can be to large-scale traversing of the landscape; while no new major surfaces were created for the drovers, the volume of livestock movement gave greater definition to many routes, as well as giving rise to sheltering enclosures for the overnight keeping of livestock and drovers' inns for the refreshment and accommodation of those leading the droves.

Droving drew to a close as the 1800s waned towards 1900, but a reference to them in 1859 shows that there were still Welsh droves in operation far from home, with grazing cattle at the Rollrights stone circle adjacent to the ridgeway road straddling the Oxfordshire and Warwickshire border.

Another type of route, the packhorse way, while easy to track in the Peak District and Pennines, is more difficult to work out and follow in the North Wales landscape. Their presence is best detected by particular bridges (see below), excepting the Roman Steps, which is something of a misnomer – the narrow metalled stepped surface is much more consistent with a tight linear procession of animals bearing packs (panniers) on their sides.

Whereas droves were formed by wide sprawls of animals moving as a body in a broad linear route, the packhorses were usually single trains of mules, travelling with laden bags. Evidence of this can be seen at the packhorse bridge over the River Alwyn at Caergwrle, north of Wrexham. A narrow causeway with a low wall meant that the saddlebags of the passing mule trains would not be damaged against a higher wall. Triangular recesses incorporated above the cutwaters of the bridge also gave limited passing places for other foot traffic. Another packhorse bridge of note is at Pont Penybenglog at the neck of the Ogwen Pass before Telford's more modern surface descends the east side of Nant Ffrancon towards Bethesda and Bangor. A careful investigation beneath the bridge reveals a single course of masonry arching over the precipice cut out by the water.

A surprising lack of evidence of saltways into North Wales stands in stark juxtaposition with the amount of salt supply routes heading north and east from Cheshire. The neighbouring English county, possessing three of England's four inland salt towns (Middlewich, Northwich and Nantwich, with Droitwich much further south in the Midlands being the fourth), was eminently well-placed to have supplied salt to its Welsh neighbours. Nantwich in particular was attacked and occupied by the Welsh on many occasions, even receiving the Welsh name of Hellath Wen. In more peaceful times Welsh visitors trading with Nantwich were accommodated overnight on the west side of the River Weaver on Welsh Row, which led on to Welshman's Lane. The only definite salt route given is that heading from Nantwich to Holt on the River Dee; after which the saltway's course is unknown. Nantwich later served as a stop on the coach road from London to Chester.

Turnpikes

Against this backdrop of growing trade and movement of livestock was the overwhelming neglect of the transport infrastructure. The Highways Act of 1555 devolved the repair and supervision of roads to local parishes; under-resourced and often without proactive attitudes, this had little effect upon even the satisfactory maintenance of the routes.

In 1663 a turnpike was first created at Wadesmill near Ware in Hertfordshire, and John Ogilby began to audit routes just over a decade later, providing a coach route map for North Wales in1682. It was not for over a century with the General Turnpike Acts of 1766 and 1773, that turnpike creation was further facilitated enabling widespread take-up.

Into the eighteenth century wealthy landowners were able to construct their own roads, such as that from Lord Penryhn's slate quarry near Bethesda – indicative of the economic dependence upon providing reliable surfaces to do the job required. Public routes remained an uncertain means of traversing the land and depended upon the role of turnpikes to reverse or improve their state.

Turnpike – a term not much used in Britain today but very prevalent in the USA – in this context refers to the barrier, spiked upon the upper side, which was placed across the road until the toll had been paid. Many tollhouses are still recognisable, with a door or window fronting directly onto the road. In Wales, the term 'tyrpeg', a contraction of 'ty'rpeg', refers to such houses – literally meaning house of the pike. Examples survive south of Pont Abeglaslyn on the Beddgelert to Porthmadog road, and on the south side of the steep descent from Bala to Llangynog in the Berwyn Mountains. Other examples will be noted below.

Given that turnpikes naturally required a toll, they were unpopular – all the more so if the fee for passage was deemed extortionate or indeed economically crippling for those needing to use them. One helpful analogy to bear in mind is the antipathy with which traffic wardens are commonly held nowadays. This is how toll-gate keepers were perceived – and happening upon them was not down to unfortunate parking and a chance discovery. To travel, one had to use the roads. Livestock, goods, crops, post – all had to face this tax. The situation exploded with the so-called "Rebecca Riots" in May 1839 in South Wales, where men dressed as women called Rebecca attacked tollhouses, barriers, and sometimes their staff. This is briefly looked at in Chapter Six.

While the creation of the Turnpike Trusts was commendable, the methodology of road construction and maintenance left much to be desired, and was something of a lottery depending on when and where the road was situated. Road surfaces were mere potholed tracks, and were in places impassable depending upon the time of year, when the course of the route may vary if the foot, horse or carriage traffic were able to delineate from the way. Into this stepped an innovative master of self-promotion, the Scotsman John Loudon MacAdam. He introduced systematic management of Turnpike Trusts and controlled, consistent practice in road construction. If not able to be involved himself, he would ensure family members were in control of many of the Turnpike Trusts, at least in the initial stages. His technique gave rise to the name for the road surface which is still with us today – tarmac, or in full, tarmacadam – though today's product, whilst still using his principle, is very much different from its original form.

This was a much needed invention, as the state of the roads was most unfortunate, though the progressing network of turnpikes was beginning to address the dire state of transport affairs; "Nobody expected it to be good going. Indeed it seems to have been generally accepted in some districts that the worst possible way between two given points was along the common road." (7)

Thomas Telford

A contemporary of MacAdam, Thomas Telford was also responsible for many of the greatest transport infrastructure creations in North Wales. His strategic revision of the route from the Midlands linking Llangollen to Betws y Coed and Bangor, the creation of the Menai Suspension Bridge, and the onward route to Holyhead for connection with Ireland, remain unsurpassed in terms of breathtaking scale.

"We may read how proudly the first London coach, the 'Oxonian', crossed the new bridge in 1826, slowing down a bit from its regulation pace of eleven miles an hour, and loaded with its dozen and a half passengers and the Irish mail-bags – the very embodiment of rapid travelling for all measurable time to come, as it surely seemed. Within twenty years Stephenson had begun that other great structure, through which a far different kind of Irish mail, bearing a very different weight of burden, was to go bounding at fifty miles an hour." (8)

As the kingdom of roads reached its first nadir, the roads would soon lose much of their traffic. The Turnpike Trusts fell victim to the same culprit as the canal network which had been constructed with almost manic determination from the 1760s to the 1820s. The age of the train was dawning, which would soon lessen the need for road and canal transport. Connections from the major rail junction at Crewe, traffic from the growing cities of Liverpool and Manchester, with Derby, Birmingham and Shrewsbury feeding into the Bangor and Holyhead rail route, and Chester as a further rail node – all meant a decrease in reliance upon the roads.

It is no coincidence that the last Turnpike Trusts were set up in 1835 and '36, and the first train passed through Crewe train station on 4th July 1837. This would soon be pivotal in opening up the North Wales coast for travellers from the Midlands and the South. Trains may not have killed the road network, but they did contribute to the fading of their pre-eminence, until motorised land transport arose with the personal motorcar. The last of the Turnpike Trusts ended in 1885, with the last tollgate closing on Anglesey in 1895.

Trains also saw to the demise of the drove routes, with livestock being taken to train stations for onward carriage to their destination. "Even before 1845, the Liverpool and Manchester line was dealing with more than 100,000 animals annually" The last drove across Wales from Aberystwyth was in 1870, with a small brief revival in 1912 during a railway strike." (9)

It is the routes from prehistory up to and including the turnpikes which will now be examined: the history of human movement and efforts to direct that movement within arguably the most breathtaking and, until the advent of modern road technology, near-impenetrable of landscapes – that of North Wales. The central arc of the Cambrian Mountains, the Berwyn and Hiraethog, the Harlech Dome, the Clwydian range and Snowdonia, with river crossings of the Dee, Conwy and the dramatic waters of the Menai Strait, among other obstacles: all are to be crossed.

CHAPTER 2

Prehistoric Trackways

Cursus Monuments

It is most unfortunate that of only two currently known definite cursus monuments in North Wales, one is now beneath an industrial estate, and the other is only available to aerial appreciation, given the correct climate and weather conditions, by way of cropmarks.

Cursus monuments elsewhere are well documented. Among the most appreciable and also the most ignored is the cursus just north of Stonehenge, delineated by plantations and subtle but recognisable parallel earthworks; from the peace of the cursus one can watch the hordes of coach parties arrive and depart, unaware of the wide Neolithic and Bronze Age landscape of which Stonehenge is a tiny centrepiece. The largest cursus is in north-east Dorset, some 10km long and the biggest Neolithic monument in Britain. North Wales does not have that to offer, but there are impressive ancient landscapes with cursus monuments, albeit interpreted with the aid of archaeological techniques, both invasive and non-invasive.

The most northerly known cursus site is at Llandegai just outside Bangor. It had an alignment of south-east to north-west, situated in relation to the later site of St Tegai's church. (1) The cursus has characteristic twin banks 14m apart, and ditches 3m wide at their top, from SH594710 to SH597710. It is visible to the informed observer for 900m. As with many cursus monuments, it is associated with another typical monument of the late Neolithic – a henge. A henge is comprised of an earthen bank and an interior ditch forming a ring with a number of possible entrances, though there are a variety of technical specialist sub-classifications. If one has a henge it would not be atypical to have

The Stonehenge Cursus; at one and three quarters of a mile long it is the second longest monument on the Stonehenge landscape. Many come so close to yet remain so far from one of these little-known but impressive Neolithic tracks across the landscape. None survive so well in North Wales. Picture marked a little to aid visibility.

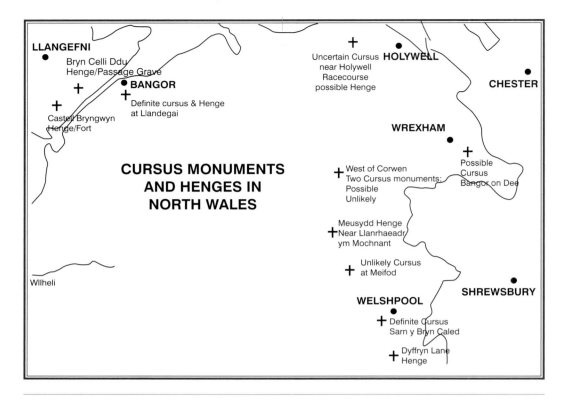

LLANGEFNI
Bryn Celli Ddu
Henge/Passage Grave

BANGOR
Definite cursus & Henge
at Llandegai

Castell Bryngwyn
Henge/Fort

Wllheli

CURSUS MONUMENTS
AND HENGES IN
NORTH WALES

Uncertain Cursus HOLYWELL
near Holywell
Racecourse
possible Henge

CHESTER

WREXHAM

Possible
Cursus
Bangor on Dee

West of Corwen
Two Cursus monuments:
Possible
Unlikely

Meusydd Henge
Near Llanrhaeadr
ym Mochnant

Unlikely Cursus
at Meifod

SHREWSBURY

WELSHPOOL

Definite Cursus
Sarn y Bryn Caled

Dyffryn Lane
Henge

Map 1

a cursus; something to be borne in mind when considering a possible henge site further east near Holywell Racecourse (below). Llandegai also has henge monuments, Neolithic houses, and many burnt mounds from later Bronze Age activity.

The other certain monument is the Welshpool Cursus, also known as Sarn-y-bryn Caled I. Crop-marks show an outline of the parallel earthworks, angled south-west to north-east, at SJ216045 to SJ218050 over 370m. In reference to modern roads, the monuments are situated in the fields roughly west of the A483/A458 roundabout just south of Powis Castle, running almost parallel to the road. Other structures and earthworks contemporary with the site reinforce its status as a cursus monument; similarly the henge complex off Dyffryn Lane to the south indicate much activity here in the late Neolithic and into the Bronze Age. The monuments' placement in a river valley is typical, with the River Severn not far to the east, and the confluence with the Camlad a little to the south.

There is a possible cursus at Tyn-y-Cefn west of Corwen, along with another more unlikely candidate (see below); the site under consideration is just 50m south of that. As is typical, two ditches 27m apart and extending 120m run south-south-west to north–north-east, with sympathetic earthworks to their north end and a Bronze Age barrow, which often feature in landscapes associated with cursus monuments, some 400m south.

In May 2007 during aerial photography cropmarks consistent with a cursus were observed south-east of Wrexham, west of Bangor Is Y Coed, at SJ369458. These ditches of an elongated enclosure extend for 200m on an east–west axis. Though not conclusive, the site is suggestive as a typical location for a late Neolithic causeway. (2)

An unlikely cursus is that at Meifod (SJ151137), north-west from Welshpool. The ditches here are 20m apart running for some 160m, but they are thought to form part of field boundaries or a later track. Another unlikely cursus near the one west of Corwen, south of Rug chapel and below the A5, is Llyn y Cefn at SJ063434. This is situated at the confluence of the rivers Alwen and Dee, where two ditches parallel to each other or almost convergent run for 400m. The terraces around rivers and confluences do lend themselves to these Neolithic monuments, but this location is thought perhaps to be field boundaries.

Another uncertain candidate is near Holywell, just south of Gorsedd. It is referred to as Ysceifiog, though Holywell Racecourse is a nearer geographical point of reference at SJ152752. Unlike all the others it is detectable with the naked eye at ground level. The ditches are 15m apart, running for 70m as they approach a large circular earthwork which has been described as a henge (3), with an off-centre burial mound containing flints dating to the early Bronze Age. Offa's Dyke is argued by some to extend north from the monument, though that single linear feature does not align with the twin ditches to the south, and does not intersect the monument. A possible designation of a long barrow is given (4), but that remains inconclusive. A hitherto explored option is that of an avenue – a ceremonial approach route as has been noted most famously at Stonehenge. There is a less well-known but equally observable example at Arbor Low in The Peak District.

Prehistoric Trackways

For the contemporary investigator of prehistoric routes, there may not seem to be that many upon which to expend one's curiosity. Tracks above Rowen, Llanbedr and Penmaenmawr are fairly obvious to the well-informed researcher. Just south of this area, Ffordd Ddu, which runs along Cadair Idris, is dense in ancient monuments and has an obvious pre-Roman route.

Longueville-Jones offers many possible routes in North-East Wales in a brief piece giving itineraries of antiquities. His criteria for recognising an ancient track are unclear. To what extent his naming of a site constitutes a recognisable "A to B" route, or a dedicated marking which may indicate recognisable linear passage in antiquity, is uncertain. Routes he proposes are as follows:

He gives a north – south route across the hills west of Gwytherin. No other details are offered, though one could suggest a route from Pennant towards Llangernyw with its ancient yew, churchyard and possible standing stones. Gwytherin's church, sited upon a mound with early mediaeval stones (and also some which could be prehistoric) may lend this credence.

From Oswestry, he offers a route to Llanarmon Dyffryn Ceiriog through Llawnt and Rhiwlas, penetrating the Berwyn west of Pentre. This is not unique in that it is the route of a later droveway. One may extrapolate a link with Cynwyd on the west side, or a descent via the Bronze Age cairn circle of Moel Ty Uchaf (SJ057371). This may well link in with a route in the Dee Valley, including the Tyfos cairn circle (SJ028388) on the west of the Dee, and Moel Ty Uchaf to Bwlch Maen Gwynedd – the Pass of the Stone of Gwynedd. The stone named here is a natural erratic serving as a prominent marker, but there is also a Bronze Age cairn of white quartz which may have served as a visible burial marker and thoroughfare in the landscape.

He also suggests a route from Chester to Bala. Recent excavations at the Chester Amphitheatre have shown evidence of Iron Age farming, and a post hole cut in to the pre-Roman bedrock on the site. Given its hilltop situation, a presence here in the first millennium BC is consistent with every other hilltop location in Cheshire. The route follows the line of Llandegla, north-east to south-west (the current route of the A5104), continuing on to Brynegwlys (with two defended settlements to the south on the spur west of the Horse Shoe Pass – Moel Gamelin (SJ176465) and Moel y Gaer (SJ167464), one of many hillforts so named) and then to the Dee Valley. A number of possible routes for this last part can be suggested: heading south past Moel Morfydd over Llantysilio Mountain, or south-west towards Carrog, or angling further west to Clawdd Poncen, which would take the route past the postulated site of a Neolithic tomb and later mediaeval boundary marker – Y Bwrdd y Tri Arglwydd (the Table of the Three Lords, SJ105468) – and the Iron Age settelement of Caer Drewyn.

Other less detailed routes listed include:

■ From Llansannan heading south-west, intersecting a ridge to Llyn Aled (convergent with a drove-way).

■ North-west over the Berwyn Mountains close to Cadair Fronwen's summit; then west to Llandrillo by Pen y Bwlch.

■ A very specific route "four miles and a half south-south-west from Nantglyn", placing it north of what is now the Lake Brenig.

■ A route south from Ysbyty Ifan (also Yspytty Evan) to Arenig Bach (Fach), the northernmost of the three Arenig summits. The way taken is via Nant y Fuddai and the Gelyn valley, on the north-east side of the mountain.

■ Pentrefoelas north-eastwards to Nantglyn, via Pen-bwlch-garnedd and Cerrig Caws.

The above ancient routes are only really identified by linking together distant monuments, settlements, and lines of best passage through the landscape (likewise the Iron Age routes given below). However, there remain two routes in North Wales which give a recognisable procession of prehistoric monuments in relatively short succession, and thus warrant an in-depth examination as Bronze Age trackways. A third is more sparse in its spread of monuments but is still recognised as a prehistoric trackway. The track from Rowen to Bwlch y Ddeufaen, a well-known trackway, is covered in depth in the chapter on Roman roads owing to the survival of much Roman agger and linear markings besides the wide array of prehistoric remains.

Llanbedr to Trawsfynydd – Fonlief Hir

The westernmost of these two routes begins at Llanbedr near the airbase of Maes Artro and the popular holiday resort of Shell Island. Much of the higher route formed the main mountain thoroughfare until the 1800s, and was the way taken by Giraldus Cambrensis in 1188. There is some ambiguity as to the name; while the Monuments Database records this as the "Fonlief Hir" trackway, the map notes it as "Fonllech Hir".

Neolithic activity in this area was intense, with a proliferation of dolmens: Dyffryn Ardudwy with its twin tombs, Cors y Gedol (SH603228), Bron y Foel Isaf (SH608246), Gwern Einion (SH587286) and another pairing at Carneddau Hengwm (SH614205). Even the Victorian structure of St Peter's Church in Llanbedr (SH585269) houses a Neolithic stone with a spiral pecked into its face – but the Bronze Age trackway begins to the north-west of the church.

In an enclosure stand two stones, "Meini Hirion" (SH583270), one wafer thin, the other a solid wedge-shaped slab. The former has questionable antiquity. It is some distance to the north-east that one may pick up the alignment of monuments heading past Gwern Einion chambered tomb, now incorporated within drystone walling. Though predating the Bronze Age route it is nonetheless indicative of earlier actitivty, and the line of best passage can remain through millennia with certain provisos.

A mile or so north of Gwern Einion, the trackway is once again defined by a series of standing stones. The first appears upon the righthand side – Carreg, with the broad low ring of a cairn to its rear. Further on, there is a more imposing megalith upon the left, with a further two diminutive stones alternating right and left. Marking the way of Bronze Age activity further up are two cairn

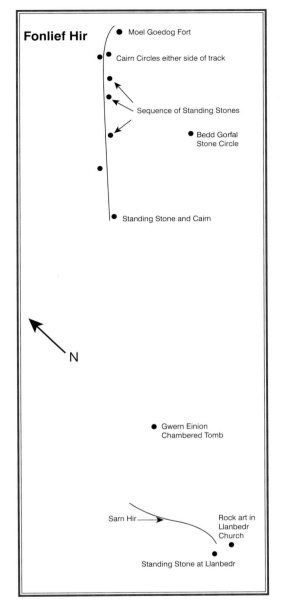

Map 2

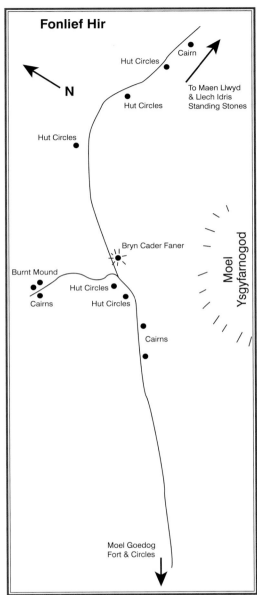

Map 3

circles (SH610325) beneath the later Iron Age ramparted settlement of Moel Goedog; these two burial monuments are the remains of two denuded burial monuments straddling and indicating the ancient route. One of the circles is visible from each respective direction of approach, suggesting contemporary design with each other. (5)

The pinnacle of the route in terms of archaeology is one of the most breathtaking ancient sites one could hope to visit. The route onward is subject to very boggy conditions with confident map-reading required; it may be hard to believe that the route was once surfaced and maintained, but having

The lower of the two cairn circles along Fonlief Hir at Moel Goedog; tidal crossing of the Glaslyn estuary, Portmeirion and Porthmadog to the rear.

Evidence of more recent surfacing on the Bronze Age trackway.

seen no serious attention since the 1700s its lack of appeal as a route to all but the most determined of walkers is understandable. Passing further Bronze Age cairns and Iron Age dwellings with varying degrees of interpretable remains, all of which testify to the ongoing use of the way through, one arrives at the prehistoric crown of megalithic thorns of Bryn Cader Faner (SH648353). Even though some of the angled slabs were removed in World War II, it remains without equal, and is unique.

Perhaps indicative of a western link to the route, cairns straddle the path descending south of Y Gyrn, and a burnt mound exists next to the stream; but the main route continues on taking the route of easiest passage around Moel Ysgyfarnogod, into Cwm Moch to the Maen Llwyd standing stone near Trawsfynydd at SH707323 and Llech Idris at SH731312, having intersected the later Roman track of Sarn Elen.

Druids' Circle and Environs

Speaking of stone circles in North Wales, Burl records: "Dates from them prove this when trade between Wales, Ireland and and England was strong. Circles on long-established track ways, standing stones guiding travellers from one to another, are records of the constant visits and departures. Axes from Graig Lwyd were plentiful in Wales and many reached Wessex, the east and west Midlands, and Yorkshire. The ways were marked. In the absence of navigable rivers men walked." (6)

This area above Penmaenmawr gives a most engaging procession of monuments, no doubt a result of of the axe works at Graig Lwyd and the Great Orme copper mines (see below) in the Neolithic and Bronze Age, respectively. It must be pointed out that the current headland at Penmaenmawr which once supplied the axe factory from its volcanic plug is nothing like that which earlier people, even up to the last couple of hundred years, would have seen. Originally it towered above the area, much like other mountains on the Lleyn Peninsula – but quarrying has robbed the enormous mountain of much of its stature once so awe-inspiring to travellers along the North Wales coast. The quarrying also completely obliterated an Iron Age hill fort.

Remains of the routes can be made out at times by hollow ways, or they are indicated by the monu-

Without equal, Bryn Cader Faner – the crown of the Bronze Age trackway into the mountains from Llanbedr to Trawsfynydd.

Maen Penddu standing stone marking the Bronze Age trackway between Conwy and Penmaenmawr.

ments which served to hold the dead, guide the living, or act as focal points for social and commercial activity. Writing of the track adjacent to the Druids' Circle, Burl notes "…the trackway that today can be made out as a hollow trail that goes directly by the north side of the bank, protected from the sea-winds by a rise in the ground. The Druids' Circle appears to have been situated at the juncture of several such tracks, a fact that points to its status as a meeting-place." (7)

On the south-east side of the area a tall standing stone, Maen Hir (the long stone, SH748750), stands alone in a field below the ruinous but clear stone circle of Hafodty (SH747752), itself bisected by a modern track, in common with other features indicative of an earlier route. Further on to the south-west, clearly adjacent to the track is the impressive monolith of Maen Penddu (SH739735). The contours of the top of the stone mimic those of the hillock behind it; whilst this is striking, the erosion of several millennia cannot have left any original shaping untouched.

Then, on the hillside to the north of the track is the clearly visible but diminutive stone circle of Cefn Maen Amor (SH738735). Any sighting of these stones now adjacent to the track is likely a free interpretation of a fortuitous. The exact ancient route across the open expanse is unclear, but further on an ancient trackway can be picked up clearly again, passing the remains of the Red Farm stone circle (SH732750), slightly downhill and south from the current track. A large amount of cairn material, possibly clearance from other Bronze Age monuments, can be seen in the field.

Continuing along the track a large natural stone, Maen Crwn (SH731750), an obvious marker stone on the left-hand side shows the way. Bearing to the right through the drystone wall, one comes across a telegraph pole planted in the top of a small mound on the right hand side – this is the Bronze Age round barrow of Fridd Wanc (SH726748). Across the way is the tiny stone circle named Circle 275

(SH725747) – five enormous pebble-like stones in a ring, showing Irish influence in a region which also shows traits typical of stone circles found in Cumbria and Scotland.

From Circle 275, the jewel in the crown of the megalithic monuments along the trackway is clear – the Druids' Circle (SH723746), standing on a shelf just south of the highest ground. The peaks of Tal y Fan beckon to the south, and the cairn-topped dome of Moelfre is to the south-west. Over a small spur of land, and completely invisible to the casual visitor unless they decide to walk south-west over the small ridge to a hollow, is another circular monument – Circle 278 (SH722746), a cairn circle. Clearly visible from the Druids' Circle to the immediate west is a confusing jumble of stones which seem to defy classification, but which are unimaginatively named Monument 280 (SH722746).

Dropping from the high land further to the north and west to an inverted 'Y'-outline pointing north in the drystone walling, once more a wishful imagination lends itself to interpret arrangements

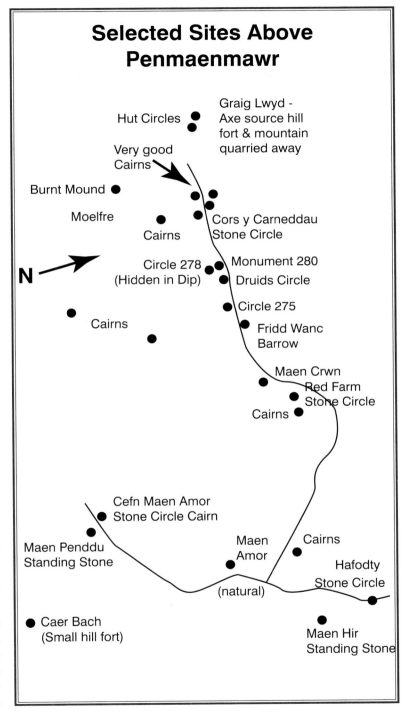

Selected Sites Above Penmaenmawr

Graig Lwyd - Axe source hill fort & mountain quarried away

Hut Circles

Very good Cairns

Burnt Mound

Moelfre

Cairns

Cors y Carneddau Stone Circle

N

Circle 278 (Hidden in Dip)

Monument 280

Druids Circle

Circle 275

Cairns

Fridd Wanc Barrow

Maen Crwn

Red Farm Stone Circle

Cairns

Cefn Maen Amor Stone Circle Cairn

Maen Penddu Standing Stone

Maen Amor

Cairns

Hafodty Stone Circle

(natural)

Caer Bach (Small hill fort)

Maen Hir Standing Stone

Map 4

of stones to form what was the stone circle of Cors Y Carneddau (SH718746). Before arriving at the denuded crags of Graig Lwyd, once the source for stone axes, another three identifiable Bronze Age monuments testify to the line of the route: a large conical hollowed-out cairn, a small ring of stones adjacent to a telegraph pole, and a much wider ring of stones from cairn kerbing (SH716747).

The extent of monuments along this route reflects the continuing practice of human activity, life and death along the axis of industrial supply and distribution routes which gave the reason for settlement as opposed to nomadic lifestyles or transhumance (alternating between upland and lowland areas depending upon climate or season). The source of important goods leaves testimony for the following and subsequent generations.

Prehistoric Trackways on Anglesey – An Exploration

The question of ancient trackways upon Anglesey is something that ought to be explored. Given the profusion of Neolithic tombs, Bronze Age standing stones, Iron Age hut circles, some hillforts (around the coast) and Romano-British settlements, the absence of obvious trackways on Ynys Mon, or of studies seeking a wider interpretation, is puzzling.

Elsewhere (for example, as with those routes considered above), a profusion of prehistoric monuments readily yields an interpretation of an ancient trackway. For Anglesey, it is certain that there was a sizeable population, at least in the Iron Age since it offered enough resistance to warrant putting down by the Romans. The sheer density of Bronze Age and Neolithic activity must surely have required reasonable-sized settlements, generating well-used routes between different familial groups or tribes upon the island. In many other places it is a demonstrable principle that standing stones were used (among other purposes) as waymarkers – especially in valley bottoms where they could confirm the right passage, or in open, featureless areas requiring points of reference. Although out of the geographical region of this book, the tallest standing stone in Shropshire at Whitcott Keysett (SO276823), now pulled down and broken into fragments, is situated on a valley floor next to a fording point on a river.

Wendy Hughes, exploring "Anglesey Past and Present", remarks upon the bounteous number of menhirs that "although their existence remains a mystery their abundance and prominent positions indicate that they were of vital significance to our ancestors." (8) Why are the stones so visible? Why can they often be viewed in conjunction, either with each other or with landscape features? One could suggest this is for the very same reason that mileposts and road signs are visible – to give guidance across a landscape. On the basis of a tall stone visible for some distance around, in tandem with other suggestive evidence, the following are examples of menhirs that could serve as trackway markers on Anglesey.

North of Llangefni is a tall roadside standing stone, on the east side of the road just opposite a school. This menhir gives the name to the hamlet just to the north: Maenaddwyn (SH461834). The stone has been progressively obscured by ivy in the last ten years, observed on repeated revisits; those unfamiliar with the area would now pass it by, mistaking it for a large tree stump. It is situated just before a line of pylons, and opposite the school with a plaque relating to the mathematical principle of pi and William Jones who was the first to use the Greek letter in relation to the mathematics behind the concept. Not far away to the north-east is Mynydd Bodafon, from where on a good day all of the island can be seen, with the wondrous framing of Snowdonia on the southern horizon. A clustering of hut circles may denote an even earlier Bronze Age presence in the area. Maenaddwyn, with its roadside siting, even having been incorporated into a wall, must have been marking this road and earlier trackway for several millennia.

A little to the south-west of Maenaddwyn stands another fine menhir, Llech Golman (SH452831). Sited on the rise of a south-west-facing incline, the distance between the two stones is not far, and

The standing stone of Maenaddwyn next to the roadside several millennia after it was first placed there; Mynydd Bodafon with its hut circles to the rear.

a relationship in terms of denoting part of a trackway is possible.

To the north-west stands a more diminutive stone with interesting associated folklore, which suggests a memory of it having served alongside a more ancient way. Carreg Leidr (the Thief Stone, SH446843) resembles a hunched figure from certain angles, and has the story associated with it of being the petrification of a thief. The tale goes that two of the island's most important saints, Saint Seiriol and Saint Cybi, would meet near this spot having journeyed from their respective parts of Anglesey, the location being equidistant for them to walk to. St Seiriol was known as St Seiriol the Fair, for in journeying from his dwelling at Penmon on the far east tip of Ynys Mon, he walked to Carreg Leidr with the sun on his back in the morning, and likewise when he walked home in the evening when the westering star was descending. St Cybi was known as St Cybi the Tanned, for he had a darker appearance. Leaving Caer Gybi (Holyhead), he walked into the light in the morning, and also faced the sun homeward-bound. This is the legend of Cybi Felyn and Seiriol Wyn.

As for the tale of the stone, the meeting of these saints is said to have conferred holiness upon the land in the area. When a thief stole a Bible from a nearby church and was making his escape complete with the swag, the holiness of the place turned him to stone for his most heinous act. The church that figures in the legend is not specified, and whether or not the Bible was returned or was petrified with him is also not related. While the folklore relates an interesting yarn, it does also suggest an ancient route in the memory of the tale.

Additionally, two forgotten holy wells nearby add weight to the suggestion of there having been a route. Whether or not this very close pairing of wells featured in any later pilgrimage, either local or wider, is unknown. West of Maenaddwyn, approaching Carreg Leidr, on either side of the approach to a bridge on the east side of a stream between Hebron and Clorach Fawr two springs once flowed. The well on the north side, Ffynnon Deiniol (SH44908416), is related to Saint Deiniol, the patron of Bangor Cathedral. –The well itself is now completely lost beneath mud and undergrowth. The well on the south side, Ffynnon Gybi (SH44908414), has fared somewhat better, though its prospects are not good. This flow is attributed to Saint Cybi and has a broken manhole cover, while a flow of water still trickles into the stream a short way away. Has the east–west route and and Lon Leidr – Thief Lane, to the west of the standing stone – been there for considerable time? The way is deeply incised into the hillside, and could be a modernised, surfaced hollow way.

Other standing stones in reasonable proximity to each other are to be found elsewhere on the island. Two stones stand in fields at Cwm Cremlyn (SH572776, SH573774); of considerable stature, they would serve as visible waymarkers in the absence of modern field boundaries and hedgerows. In a pass to the north, a small standing stone west of Llanddona (SH567796) is lost nowadays in undergrowth. The pass is very reminiscent of the Bwlch y Ddeufaen, but on a much less grand scale. The stone is south-west of a place simply named Bwlch – pass. A pair of Neolithic chambers in a collapsed state are sited west of the Cremlyn stones, south of the B5109 between Hendrefor and Ucheldref (SH551773).

North of Menai Bridge, two stones are sited upon the rises either side of the lower Cwm Cadnant (Pen-y-Maen at SH564739 and Ty-Gwyn at SH554739). There is also a further ruined Neolithic chamber, Ty Mawr, at SH539722 on the southern ridge right next to the A5025 heading east from Llanfairp-wllgwyngyll. Two more chambers demarcate a line within the grounds of Plas Newydd – one on the cricket pitch (SH520697), and the other the massive mound of Bryn yr Hen Bobl (the Hill of the Old People, SH518690). Opposite on the mainland, the standing stone of Cader Elwa (SH542683) is suggestive, and north of Bryn yr Hen Bobl, the henge-cum-passage grave of Bryn Celli Ddu (SH507702) has a standing stone to its north (Tyddyn Bach (SH503703)), with a rock outcrop – a gorsedd with Neolithic cup markings – between the stone and the grave. The proximity of the outcrop, especially with its cup marks, indicates a significant relationship between the two ancient sites.

Bypassing or crossing the expanse of the Malltraeth Marsh which penetrates far inland from Mall-traeth Bay and sands is a problem which not only the Romans, the coach road, Telford and the new A55 road have had to deal with. On the lower reaches of the land descending to the marsh, south-east from Llangefni, a standing stone around 26m above sea level south of Lledwigan (SH456740) points across the northern edge of the marsh to another stone about 23m above sea level, near Hirdre Faig (SH484745). This suggests two points indicating the shortest, easiest circumnavigation of boggy land.

To the other end of the island, south-west from Amlwch and south-east from Cemaes, two more large menhirs could work well as pointers. The towering standing stone at Bodewryd (SH406902) could be used as a marker to head north to the summit at Ysgellog, from which point there is a further stone showing in the distance at Werthyr (SH415929), with its ten-feet-tall stone reaching above the landscape. A further stone is supposed to have existed in close proximity here. A round barrow on level land at SH413918 lies between the two stones – and a viable trackway line across the landscape would appear to be confirmed.

North of Llanfechell the Meini Hirion (the Long Stones, SH364917), a trio of stones on the crest of a hill, are visible for some distance around; intervisibility can be a useful tool in working out possible relationships. The single broad slab of another standing stone just to the north-east of the village (SH370916) yields mutual visibility with the Long Stones – which incidentally are a unique arrangement of menhirs, and most surprisingly, they are devoid of any folklore or myth. The ruin-

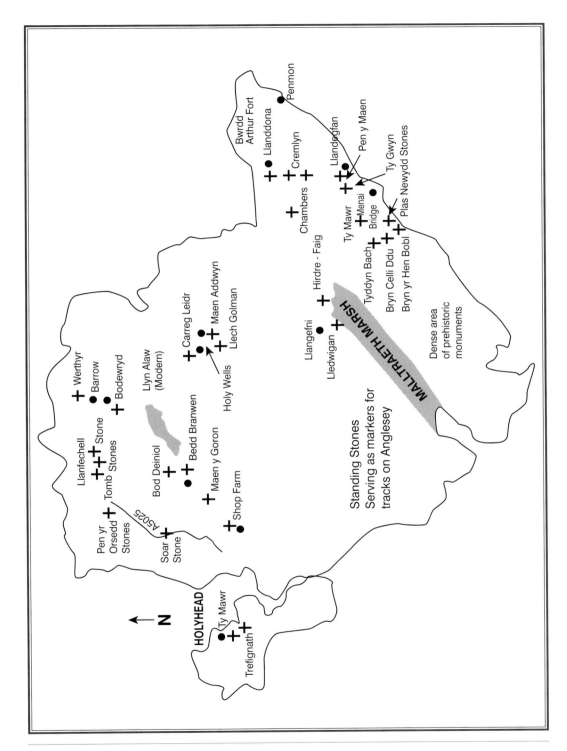

Map 5

ous remains of a Neolithic chamber are on the hill to the north-west of Y Meini Hirion at Foel Fawr (SH360920).

On land west of Pen-y-groes with a 62m contour line, and east of Mynydd y Garn with its high-point of 170m, are two tall stones standing near each other in a much wider expanse of lower land (SH333904, SH333907). The A5025 runs to the east of these large menhirs at Pen yr Orsedd. The more southerly stone is inside and near a field boundary with its northern correspondent in the middle of a field, but still visible from the lane a short way away. Is a line of easy passage between the higher land on either side being suggested by their presence?

Yet another stone, the Soar Stone at Llanfaethlu (SH319864) sits immediately upon the east side of the road – almost upon the highest point of its hill, only overtopped by the more recent chapel to its rear. This would have been easily visible for some way around, and like Maenaddwyn, its roadside situation suggests that it marks a much older trackway.

A gathering of stones south-west from Llyn Alaw suggest a passage across the Afon Alaw, though Llyn Alaw is a man-made reservoir and obviously would not have been part of the Bronze Age land-scape in which the stones were first placed.

Beginning at Llanynghenedl at the confluence of the B5109 and A5025 (the old coach road, though that is relatively very modern in context of this possible ancient trackway), there is a stumpy, squat standing stone in a field just north of Shop Farm (SH318813). Taking a line north-east a track passed between the higher ground of Llanllibio Fach and Llanllibio Fawr (to the north-west and south-east respectively). A track which emerged on the tallest hill (marked 42m) centred between these rises then would have presented from its summit a view of a likely pairing of two standing stones to the north-east (SH340832). Only one of these stones now stands erect, albeit held together in three pieces by enormous iron braces, with the other stone prostrate nearby. This is known as Maen y Gored, Maen y Goron, or Tre-gwehelydd by different sources. It is situated close to a tributary of the Afon Alaw.

Maintaining a line north-west to the next highest ground (43m, and visible from the previous high ground which is south-east from Elim), there is guidance from the decreasing contours of the land towards Anglesey's most famous Bronze Age barrow. This is Bedd Branwen (SH361850), the grave attributed to Branwen of the Mabinogion– (the collection of early mediaeval Welsh stories), with significant finds of urns discovered here during excavations. Bedd Branwen sits just above a southward curve of the Afon Alaw. To the north-east there is a tall standing stone on rising ground west of Bod Deiniol (SH368857), which marks the end point of this projected trackway.

There are many more standing stones and monuments from the Bronze Age and the Neolithic upon Anglesey, all which can help give pointers to ancient tracks upon one of the most compelling islands for the prehistorian to study. The above is merely a superficial exploration of an area which should readily attract more research. The south-west of the island is particularly dense in monuments; with the projected Roman route running past many of them (see Chapter Three), it is not unreasonable to suggest the Romans may well have been adopting an already well-used passage. The logic driving the assumption that clustering of Bronze Age remains through landscapes show trackways of that period, and maybe even older, needs to be extended and more widely applied; Anglesey provides a relatively easy subject to further such studies by virtue of the density of its megalithic remains.

The Axe Trade and Copper Mining

The Neolithic and Bronze Age supported their respective industries as human innovations in tech-nology advanced, as the names for the historical periods suggest. Two major sources supplying the raw materials for these advances were from North Wales. Seams of a mineral known now as augite granophyre were discovered at Graig Lwyd above Penmaenmawr, and were used in the manufacture of stone axe heads which were distributed all over Britain. This may go some way to explaining the concentration of megalithic monuments in the vicinity. There was also quarrying of the mineral picrite at Cwm Mawr axe factory near Hyssington east of Montgomery, and some at Mynydd Rhiw on the Lleyn Peninsula at SH234299. Of these three quarry sites, only the latter is identifiable as a Neolithic site. Graig Lwyd has continued to be quarried though not for volcanic material for axe heads, and the exact location of Cwm Mawr (Hyssington) has yet to ascertained. (9)

The Great Orme is the most famous of the Welsh copper mines, and the earliest of the known copper mining sites in Europe (around 1860 BC). However, copper was also being extracted in prehistory at Parys Mountain near Amlwch nearly two millennia before the Romans came to capitalise upon the mineral resources of Anglesey. While Parys Mountain has been closed to large-scale industry since its eighteenth century heyday (though it looks likely that commercial mining enterprise will soon return to the vicinity), and it is certainly not accessible to the public, the Great Orme mines have been opened making them a worthwhile attraction to visit. With materials from the mine having ended up far and wide in Britain and beyond, networks of roads and trackways must have been in existence to enable the endeavour to grow to the extent it did in the Bronze Age.

Hillforts

As noted, hillforts are nearly always close to the coast, or above river valleys; if there was no running water within the settlement (a few do have their own springs, even now), a supply of water needed to be found nearby. The guardianship of strategic passages seems to be an obvious function of their siting, affording views of valleys and other hilltop locations visible for miles around. This can be demonstrated by the row of forts on the Clwydian Range (see below), Conwy Mountain hillfort above the Sychnant Pass, Tre'r Ceiri on the north neck of the Lleyn Peninsula, and Llwyn Bryn Dinas in the Tanat Valley. Many others could be listed. The principle of a hilltop settlement, either temporary or permanent, was not new in the Iron Age. Some locations under excavation have yielded evidence of Mesolithic hunters having used the site millennia beforehand, and the amount of activity upon hilltops in the Bronze Age by way of barrows and cairns would mean that settlement sites would not be far distant. When Iron Age hillforts were being developed in the first millennium BC, many of the Bronze Age monuments came to be sited within the ramparts of the ancient British fortifications. (10)

The Clwydian Range

Six hillforts across the Clwydian Range form a chain of defended settlements in the north-east corner of Wales. South to north they are Moel Fenlli, Moel y Gaer (Llanbedr), Moel Arthur, the vast and impressive Penycloddiau –(one of the largest hillforts in Wales), Moel y Gaer (Bodfari), and Moel Hiraddug. Given a chain of settlements, one expects routes interconnecting them and beyond.

Longueville-Jones suggests a prehistoric route network around these Clwydian sites, which would be comparable to the 'ladder' of Roman roads either side of the Pennine ridge, interlinked at intervals to connect the north–south arterial routes by east–west 'rungs': "There is every reason to believe that two ancient roads ran, one on the east, the other on the west, side of the Vale of Clwyd, below the high grounds, from the upper part of the vale towards the sea, nearly coincident with the actual lines of road passing through the villages and towns." He suggests a route from what would now be Mold to Ruthin through Bwlch Pen Barras, to the north of Moel (also Foel) Fenlli; a route to the south of this hillfort is offered, with the suggested misnomer of Bwlch Agricola. The use of the obvious low pass in earlier periods is supported by the find of a polished black stone hammer. (11)

Moel y Gaer (Llanbedr) co-guards the passage of Bwlch Pen Barras, but due to its low position has

Bwlch Pen Barras – The east–west pass between two of the hillforts on the Clwydian Range (Foel Fenlli at the top of the hill to the left); the photo looks west towards Ruthin.

no visibility to the east, where the mass of Moel Famau obstructs the view. Moel Arthur is decisively placed: "It directly commands the col of another of the main passes through the hills at Bwlch y Ffrainc…sited to control access through the Range from east to west – this is a strategic hillfort par excellence." (12)

Examination of the villages at the possible end points of contemporary minor (and some not so minor) routes suggest tracks across the spine of the Clwydian Range. There is a possible route between Tremerchion and Pen y Cefn, and the path from Bodfari to Afon Wen would be kept in check by the northern Moel y Gaer as the river Chwiler joins the Vale of Clwyd (an easier thoroughfare, as utilised by modern roads and the now-defunct rail link). Llangwyfan to Nannerch is certainly overseen by Penycloddiau, and working south there are other routes such as Llandyrnog to Hendre, Llangynhafal to Rhydymyn, Llanfair Dyffryn Clwyd to Llanarmon yn Ial via Moel Llanfair and Llandegla to Bwlchgwyn.

Moel Hiraddug at the northern tip of the range is a stunning hillfort, albeit marred considerably upon the side near Dyserth owing to one third of the hill having been quarried away. The site has yielded considerable and notable archaeological finds from the La Tene Celtic culture. One find of a horse harness-mount shows reliable evidence of horse and pony usage from around 450 BC (13). A breathtaking plaque with a triskele may have come from a chariot, and forms the logo of the Clwyd

Powys Archaeological Trust. One must surmise that equestrian usage of these pre-Roman routes must have been part of Iron Age British life.

Other significant linking sites across the extremities of the Clwydians are yet another Moel y Gaer (Rhosemor) hillfort to the east, and Caer Drewyn at the southern limit above the bend in the Dee Valley.

In the south-east of the mountain reaches, Llanarmon yn Ial is significant as a meeting place of five routes, and is the conjectured site of a 'great Pagan centre' – a stone circle upon which the church of St Garmon was later constructed. Bwlch Crug-Glas is one of the names ascribed to the area – the Pass of the Green Mounds (14). Investigation of the chuchyard does yield some suggestive evidence. It is circular or 'sub-circular', as are many ancient churchyards in Wales, and inside the northern perimeter tucked close behind the wall are some limestone slabs out of character with the rest of the wall. However, there remains no solid archaeological evidence at this time to support the stone circle supposition, as appealing as it may be. The location certainly remains a significant conjunction of routes from Garreg Lwyd, Moel Llanfair and Moel y Plas, Llanferres, Eryrys and Mold, Graianrhyd, and Llandegla to the south. A handful of tumuli through the area, and Neolithic remains from Tomen y Faerdre on the east approach, show activity predating and contemporary with a potential stone circle at the meeting of the ways.

One modern sign one will see throughout Wales is "Dim Palmant" – "No Pavement". Palmant also signifies a paved surface in place names, and has been associated with Roman roads (Chapter Three). North of Llanarmon yn Ial and stretching from Four Crosses to Eryrys is Nant-y-Palmau, previously known as Nant-y-Palment, or the paved valley. It has been suggested this 'paving' is more down to its usage as a thoroughfare through the centuries and millennia rather than because of a deliberately metalled surface, with the innumerable footfalls upon its surface smoothing and compacting the stones and rock beneath. (15)

The activity of prehistoric Britain created roads and trackways across North Wales, forming routes used by generations over the following millennia, from the Romans, pilgrims, drovers, and today's walker and in places, the motorist, too.

CHAPTER 3

Roman Roads

An ongoing presence in Wales was essential for the Romans given that the complete pacification of the British had taken four decades and as many concerted efforts. Their presence had to be substantial enough so that any rumours of new insurgency could be promptly communicated and comprehensively extinguished, but not so large as to drain resources from elsewhere. Maintaining these garrisons and vexilations of auxiliary forces to see to any of the tribes or elements hostile to Roman occupation required a road and fortress network to keep supplies and communications open, and as was the way of Rome, these networks were brought into line with more Roman style, albeit in a rather piecemeal way throughout North Wales. It is important to bear in mind that not all of the forts and roads existed completely and simultaneously as a widely-managed system linked with continually manned settlements.

Crucial to the control of the territory was the legionary fortress at Chester – one of three in Britain, the others being Eboracum (York) and Isca (Caerleon, the city of the legion). Situated on the sandstone outcrop on the mid-Cheshire ridge, commanding views were afforded in many directions, especially to the west towards the Clwydian Range and its network of British forts across the northern gateway to the land. The town of Chester was then situated strategically at the lowest fording place on the River Dee, allowing its use as a port. Akin to King Edward's fortresses being open to naval access 1100 years hence, Chester (or Deva, after the Dee) could keep supply routes open via the Dee estuary. Until Liverpool overtook Chester as a port and the Dee silted up close to Chester, the city commanded land and sea routes across the Wirral peninsula and the North Welsh coastline.

Shortly after the foundation of the fort of Chester, other forts to hold auxiliary units were put into place at distances suitable for men to march. Canovium and Segontium were the principal forts across the northern line of occupation. Many of the Roman forts tend to derive their name from the rivers upon which they were sited, and these two are no exception. Canovium is named after a variant of the River Conwy, and Segontium after the Seiont. (Other examples are Ribchester, Doncaster, Derby (Derventio, after the Derwent), Exeter and Caerleon (Roman name Isca, after the Usk)).

On the neck of the Lleyn Peninsula was the small fort of Pen Llystyn. Between Capel Curig and Betws y Coed was Caer Llugwy, south-east of the approach to the Ogwen Pass. Further along a projected route south was Tomen y Mur near Trawsfynydd (which even has the remains of such Roman culture as an amphitheatre); further south still to the southern geographical limit of this work is the fort at Brithdir, north-east of Dolgellau.

Taking a dog-legged route through the centre of the region, there were forts at Caer Gai on the south-west of Llyn Tegid (or Lake Bala), and also slightly further north-east near Llanfor, with a further military encampment north-east from Ruthin.

Controlling the eastern borders, Mediolanum (now Whitchurch in Shropshire) was the midway point travelling north from Wroxeter to Chester. Further west and slightly south, the significant fortress at Rhyn Park (near Chirk) kept watch over the approach to the Dee Valley towards Llangollen, a site which is itself near the important Iron Age hillfort at Llanymynech with its deposits of lead and copper.

Temporary camps, also known as marching camps, are noted at Penygwryd, west from Betws y Coed near the Llanberis Pass, Derwydd-bach near Pen Llystyn; south from Caer Gai at Rhyd Sarn, and west of Llanfor. There is another at Penrhos nestling at the confluence of the rivers Dee and Alwen west of Corwen, on a strategic convergence of several routes. There are in excess of ten practice camps in the region of Tomen y Mur at Llyn Hiraethlyn and Dolddinas.

Contained in this clear network of Roman communications is the question of the location of a fort mentioned in the Antonine Itinerary – Varis, situated to the east of St Asaph. This would have provided a stopping-off point between Deva and Canovium. The definite location is not know, although a position somewhere just east of the river is favoured. The remains of a Roman hypocaust on the edge of Prestatyn is testimony to the ongoing presence and movement of Romans with their attendant culture and comforts.

Until recently the lack of Roman roads on Anglesey had been a puzzle given the widespread finds indicative of Roman activity. The Gwynedd Archaeological Trust (GAT) had been engaged in extensive research from desktop studies to field research, and proposes two main Roman routes on Anglesey: one from the Menai Bridge area arcing to the north-east whilst progressing across the island; the other from a landing point opposite Caernarfon concluding at Holyhead.

A fort beneath modern-day Aberffraw is also proposed on the basis of excavations in the early 1970s, but given that the area concerned is now under a very heavily built-up part of the town, further investigative and confirmatory work is not likely for some time. The town's important role as the capital of Anglesey into the mediaeval period perhaps lends weight to there having been an earlier key operation on the site. The well known late sea fort at Holyhead (Caergybi) still stands in part, with Roman masonry still in existence around the later but still very ancient church. This fort would have had immediate access to the dock with a much nearer seafront than today. Further Romano-British settlements at Din Lligwy and Caer Leb and the Parys Mountain copper mines, in concert with a profusion of early mediaeval gravestones, demonstrate the spread of Latin and Roman culture through Mon Mam Cymru.

The first general research into Roman roads in North Wales was by Thomas Codrington in 1903, with the most definitive statement on the subject by Ivan Margary, who published works and subsequent revisions in 1955, 1967, and 1973. Edmund Waddelove has produced superb work, namely his 1999 tome detailing 'recent discoveries', which is received with a qualified but enthusiastic welcome. In recent years both of the archaeological trusts for North Wales, CPAT for Powys and North Wales east of the river Conwy, and GAT for Gwynedd and Anglesey west of the River Conwy, have undertaken considerable fresh research, with desktop studies and time in the field examining the possibilities of the Roman network. The serious student would do well to spend time consulting the reports in depth at their offices in Welshpool and Bangor respectively.

Tracing the routes needs to be done with qualification. In reading this section on Roman roads, it is helpful to bear in mind that "Tidy as these are, they are misleading in practice. The courses of few, if any, roads are known in their entirety, and alternative lines for some have been proposed and argued over, yet have never been properly resolved." (1) So, while presenting an apparently comprehensive picture, many of the routes are projected. There will be amendments and corrections to data in the future.

Following Roman routes where remains can be seen on the ground can be problematic in determining an exact date. As with all roads, their substructure and their surfaces need ongoing repairs, or periodic adjustments off the original course subject to immediate conditions and events – climate, storms, or demands placed on the road by the extent (or lack) of its use. A route which has not been adopted for contemporary usage may well have seen many divergent and convergent ways along the same axis over time, making interpretation uncertain. Dating the roads to which period of the Roman occupation they were constructed or principally used in is even more so. Dating evidence or historical annotation somewhere is needed. With the use and reuse of a stretch of road, different quality of materials and methods used will cause problems for the researcher. A milepost is often helpful, but may have been removed from its original context. Likewise a Roman coin is the holy grail of dating evidence, provided it is in its stratigraphic context, and that it has not been removed from its original layer in the road surface (or at the side of the original road) by weather, beast, or human prior to its discovery.

There have developed a range of different names for the same sites. Therefore, to improve clarity and reduce verbiage Segontium will be used interchangeably with its modern name of Caernarfon, likewise Deva and Chester. Caer Llugwy will be used for the fort near Betws y Coed, but some works know it as Bryn y Gefeiliau. Canovium is used to refer to the fort south of Conwy, also known as Caerhun.

Deva to Canovium

The road from Chester is in places one of the easiest to interpret. Leaving the fortress by the the south and crossing the Dee, the road would have quickly angled to the north-west, hugging the Dee estuary along the north-east Flintshire coast. It travelled above Saltney, Connah's Quay, Deeside, Flint, Bagillt and then angled westwards away from the coast at Greenfield Valley, having intersected the present-day A528 and A5121. Heading towards Carmel and Gorsedd, the Roman route cuts across and later joins the course of the modern A5026.

Of note around Gorsedd are the numbers of Bronze Age round barrows – a good number of them close by and some immediately adjacent to the route in question. At Gorsedd church there used to be two standing stones near the church, but both have been moved; one now resides in the front of a garden nursery business adjoining the church boundary to the west, and the other is much further south in the garden of a private house. Not far from here is the possible site of the cursus and henge monument at Holywell Racecourse, referred to in Chapter One.

Without any archaeological or historical evidence at all is a legend which places the site of Boudicca's last stand against the Romans in the area south of Gop Hill, not far from the high early cross of Maen Achwyfan, west from Gorsedd towards Trelawnyd. Local fields are named "Cydio ar Leni", meaning 'Seizing Legions', and a Latin-inscribed tombstone now in Whitford Church is thought to be the British resistance leader's

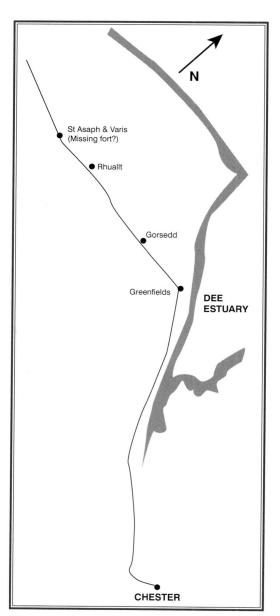

Map 1

headstone, although there is no evidence for this. (2)

The Roman line in parallel with the A5026 from Gorsedd runs convergent with the A55 Expressway, passing a tumulus on a ridge on the south side of the modern road (perhaps used as a sighting point in aligning the ancient route) before intersecting it and heading south-west in typical linear fashion. Further on it again intersects the Expressway just before Rhuallt as it descends from the northern end of the Clywdian Range towards St Asaph. Somewhere in this vicinity east of St Asaph is Varis, the 'missing' Roman fort which would have formed a staging post between Deva and Canovium.

In his exhaustive book of the period, "The Prehistoric and Roman Remains of Flintshire" Davies mentions an "Ancient Road" on Summer Hill recorded in July 1932: "The road in question leads from Summer Hill, which is less than ¼m. west of Tremeirchion church, in a N.W. direction towards Ty Moel, a distance of about ¼m. From Ty Moel it heads towards St. Asaph, but its character changes... This road is extensively paved with large slabs of limestone, with smaller stones between. Its width is about 8ft. In places the slabs show signs of considerable wear." (3)

Continuing west from St Asaph, the striking linearity of the way from Glascoed Road (SH032738) makes for easy tracing of the route, which after Sarn Rug on the south side of the modern surface (SH972743) becomes more confused by deviations. The proposed descent to the Conwy crossing is by way of a complex detour to avoid more difficult land followed by navigation towards the favoured departure point (SH797726) west of a small round hill north-west from where Bodnant Garden is today. From this hill a good view across the river is possible for a lookout. The hill's gentle slopes but clearly elevated position in context of the land around would afford a safe waiting place for any low-tide fording of the Conwy, with an obvious tactical advantage in the event of a skirmish. (4) The current and historic crossing at Tal y Cafn is just to the south-west. It is assumed that the Roman route follows an earlier course, as is opined by Longueville-Jones: "there is every reason to suppose that it was an ancient British ford, being one of the very few over the Conwy, below Llanrwst" (5). The nearby Neolithic chamber of Hendre Waelod (also known as Allor Moloch, SH793747) further up on the east bank would indicate usage as a thoroughfare before the Romans adopted it as their own specific location. Having crossed the Conwy, the fort of Canovium is a short way to the south and west.

The course of the Roman road from Gorsedd to Rhuallt as most now see it, where it intersects the A55 Expressway.

The siting of the fort of Canovium has obvious strategic significance, being at the upper tidal reach of the Conwy. It was instigated by Agricola as part of his AD 77–8 campaign against the Ordovices who had been resisting Roman occupation for over thirty years. It was an incident between the Romans and the Ordovices on the east of the Conwy at Bryn Euryn (SH832798) which acted as the catalyst for the final put-down of any British insurgency. Initially constructed with earth and timber (a common practice for longer term bases), Canovium fort was rebuilt in the middle of the second century – possibly with a dock to enable naval access at high tide. There are uneven surfaces to the south of the fort, which is a situation in keeping with there having been a civilian settlement outside of the military camp which would have provided a range of services to those garrisoned within. Cremation burials are known to have been interred to the north and south of the fortress, with horrea – granaries – over what is now the car park adjacent to the church.

In speaking of the River Conwy a concept which should be borne in mind is that it was not simply another river to cross, but was a frontier boundary. The difference in terrain on either side of the Conwy is striking. The ability of the mountains to aid resistance to any incoming force is unparalleled – something which would be experienced again and again in the post-Roman era. This, combined with the tidal nature and breadth of the lower reaches of the river, gives it the Conwy a role within Wales without equal north of the Severn estuary. Senior explains it succinctly: "The land between the Conwy and the Dee is more fertile, richer, and consequently more desirable. It is also easier to overrun. The inner sanctuary of Gwynedd is a hard country to live in, but easy to defend. The Conwy lies between them… Crossing it, historically, had psychological as well as geographical connotations… The whole social and political history of North Wales has been affected by the fact that the Conwy river is where it is. Few rivers of its size can have had so much impact on their area's history." (6)

Map 2

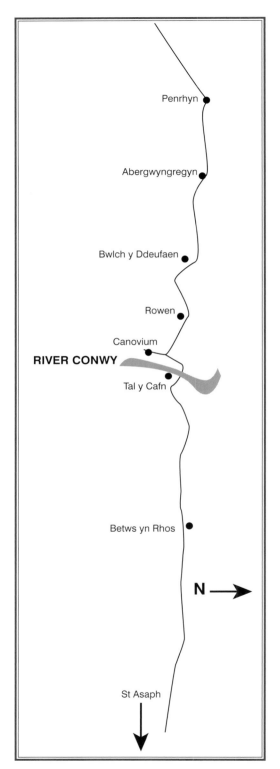

The course of the Roman road along the modern B5381 as it straddles the county boundaries.

Looking downstream on the River Conwy – not only a river but a frontier for the Romans. Taken from the present and historic Tal y Cafn crossing point.

Canovium to Segontium with the Prehistoric Trackway above Rowen

Leaving Canovium fort to the north, a line projects north-east of Ty'n-y-groes; once level with the B5279, this Roman road follows the course of the minor road (which still takes the easiest passage) to Rowen. Cutting across the top of the 'Y' formed by the roads in Rowen, the road begins a steep ascent, but without the tight hairpin bends which confound many motorists visiting the hostel there nowadays. Just north-east of the hostel the Roman route takes the same line as a (very) minor track. This stretch of road from the Rowen youth hostel to the Bwlch y Ddeufaen – the Pass of the Two Stones – is arguably without equal in terms of the surviving visibility of a Roman route not incorporated into a modern surface, and for the staggering wealth of monuments from four to two millennia before the Romans adopted the route. There are occasional indications of its later usage for the well-informed and carefully observant eye. For an introduction to investigating ancient routes this does serve as a most rewarding example.

Having served as a major Roman route, there was an attempt to turn the way through the Bwlch y Ddeufaen into a turnpike around 1769. However, this proved to be too difficult, with favour falling instead upon the more northerly route through the Sychnant Pass while still avoiding the coastal route west of Conwy. Even so, some of the later coaches for a while took this route. Today, visitors

Looking uphill along the prehistoric and Roman route above Rowen; note the earthworks on the left of the wall and the course of the track, now a hollow way.

using the approach from Rowen village to the hostel (close by where the Roman road becomes apparent) will find their last ascent has a steep bend which can prove a challenge to all but the most determined, experienced or lucky drivers. As with the Romans and the ancient British, pedestrian ascent seems more prudent.

West of Rowen youth hostel, much of the Roman route runs concurrent with the existing hollow way eroded into the mountainside; the newer route almost certainly follows the alignment of the imperial way. On the south side of the wall and underneath it, the ridge of the Roman route becomes obvious as time takes its toll in eroding the earth and stone beneath. Once the earthworks are recognised, keeping track of the way is not difficult since megalithic remains punctuate the way quite regularly. There is no doubt that the Romans were not the first to adopt this route.

The first megaliths on the pre-Roman route are in a field boundary to the north of the track at SH741718. They consist of a well-disguised standing stone, with a partner to its east. To the north-west of the line of the wall is a solitary hawthorn (used as a point of reference), and north-west again at SH741719 is a chambered tomb, very well concealed. Here there is a box-like chamber facing east, with what looks like a horned forecourt area. This is reminiscent of the Cotswold-Severn tombs and raises the question of this being of the same type. Further uphill to the north-east is a Bronze Age burial monument with a well-preserved central cist (a box for a burial; cist is also the Welsh word for a box); this is Ffrith y Ddwyffrwd at SH743723.

Continuing westward, the archetypal

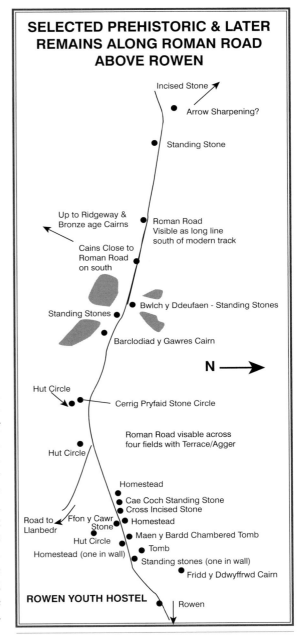

SELECTED PREHISTORIC & LATER REMAINS ALONG ROMAN ROAD ABOVE ROWEN

Incised Stone

Arrow Sharpening?

Standing Stone

Up to Ridgeway & Bronze age Cairns

Roman Road Visible as long line south of modern track

Cains Close to Roman Road on south

Bwlch y Ddeufaen - Standing Stones

Standing Stones

Barclodiad y Gawres Cairn

N →

Hut Circle

Cerrig Pryfaid Stone Circle

Roman Road visable across four fields with Terrace/Agger

Hut Circle

Homestead

Cae Coch Standing Stone
Cross Incised Stone

Road to Llanbedr | Ffon y Cawr Stone

Homestead

Maen y Bardd Chambered Tomb

Hut Circle

Tomb

Homestead (one in wall)

Standing stones (one in wall)

Fridd y Ddwyffrwd Cairn

ROWEN YOUTH HOSTEL

Rowen

Map 3

poetic picture of what a cromlech should be approaches on the right hand side (Maen y Bardd, or the Poet's Stone at SH740717). This monument also serves as part of a pasture boundary with the drystone walling incorporating the earlier structure and utilising probable cairn material which would once have concealed the arrangement of stones. A little further on the left-hand side there is a curve in the wall on the south side – this is on the perimeter of part of an Iron Age homestead.

Keeping with the earthworks associated with the Roman route on this south side of the wall, there

The course of the Roman road across the fields towards the Conwy valley – clearly delineated by the lack of growth of gorse along the course of the buried ditches.

is a ridge of earth at the edge of which is situated another standing stone of debated date. It is widely assumed to be prehistoric, although its archaeological record cites it as possibly mediaeval. It has a couple of names: Picell Arthur (Arthur's Spear); or Ffon y Cawr (the Giant's Staff, after a giant who hurled a spear at his lazy dog but missed; as is often seen with giant or diabolical hurlings, they were a poor shot). This is at grid reference SH738717. While taking note of these older monuments the causeway of the Roman route, or associated parts thereof, meanders slightly on and off the course of the contemporary way.

Near a property called Cae Coch there is an impressive oval standing stone. This is known as the Giant's Shoe – one assumes that having missed the dog with his spear, the enraged giant then removed his shoe to lob in the general direction of the hound. The standing stone is well worth a closer look at SH736716, and to its rear is yet another Iron Age homestead. Just before the standing stone, take careful examination of a stone incorporated into the bank immediately next to the track, as it has a mediaeval cross incised upon its face. There is a recent cross harshly engraved on the same stone, not to be mistaken for the very subtle remaining contours of the earlier example above it, indicative of the continued usage of the way into the post-Roman period as a place for the pilgrim or traveller to reflect upon their journey.

Heading west uphill before the tarmac surface of the route from Llanbedr y Cennin joins the track from Rowen, the Roman route departs beneath the drystone walling on the north side. The agger remains clearly visible and can be traced through a large rectangular field and onward through the next three fields. The growth of gorse also delineates the route, especially on the south side of the causeway, as its absence indicates the continued disturbance of the ground surface in a manner akin to the way cropmarks show up as diagnostic indicators on aerial photography. Viewed from the field above looking back east, the appearance is striking.

Westwards the Roman road then cuts a terrace above the tarmac lane; looking down, the small stones of the Bronze Age stone circle known as Cerrig Pryfaid (the Circle of the Flies) at SH724713 can be made out on the other side of the lane, with an outlying stone to the west. The line of the Roman road can also be clearly seen from the circle. The current lane does intersect the line of the Roman route in places, but the older route curves away from the tarmac across the field, with a clear hollow way showing the imperial road leading down to what is now the approach to the car park. The drystone wall then intersects the progression of the line of the Roman road.

This takes the ancient road to the modern car park. Just past the car park (SH719716) a Roman milestone was discovered in 1954, dating from the reign of Constantine the Great in the early fourth century. Concerning milestones, this route has been relatively rich in finds. Two earlier stones at SH679727 were found, both in good condition and of commendable workmanship; of these, one is dated to Hadrian in 121 AD, and the other to Severus in 208 AD.

The Hadrianic stone is cylindrical with script clearly incised upon the pillar. Roman milestones (and also tombstones) have their own particular style of Latin shorthand, requiring much interpretation for the unfamiliar. The inscription for this one reads:

IMP CAES TRAI
ANVS HADRIANVS
AVG P M TR P V
P P COS III
A KANOVIO / M PVIII

In fully fleshed-out Latin script this reads:

IMPERATOR CAESAR
TRAIANUS HADRIANUS
AUGUSTUS PONTIFEX MAXIMUS
TRIBUNICIA POTESTATE V
PATER PATRIAE CONSUL III
A KANOVIO MILIA PASSUM VIII

Which translates as:

"The Emperor Caesar Trajanus Hadrianus Augustus High Priest, with Tribunican power for the fifth time, Father of his Country, Consul for the third time, from Canovium 8 Miles."

On the higher field the Roman road is sometimes seen as a large curved causeway, as here in front of the drystone wall.

The stone dated to the reign of Severus is slightly thinner, with only the upper portion of the text surviving, and is thus inscribed following a similar formula:

IMP.P.CAES
L.SEP.SEVERUS
P.P.ET.M.AVR
ANTONINUS
AVGG.ET.P

In full Latin:

IMPERATORS CAESAR
LUCIUS SEPTIMUS SEVERUS
PATER PATRIAE ET MARCUS
AURELIUS
ANTONINUS
AUGUSTI ET PUBLIUS SEPTIMIUS
GETA, NOBILISSIMUS CAESAR

Which translates into English:

"The Emperor, Caesar Septimus Severus, Father of his Country, Augustus, and Marcus Aurelius Antoninus, Augustus and Publius Septimius (Geta, most noble Caesar…)

Another stone found further west, just east of Nant y Felin-fach river at SH669734, dates to the reign of Postumus in 262, having been turned upside down and put into secondary use a grave-stone probably in the fifth century – possibly for the grave of a Saint or Chieftain with the Latinised pre-Roman name of Dinoconsuodicus. This stone is very rough and unfinished in appearance. The Roman inscription is

MO
PIG FE
L AVG
PMC
TP P-O-O
T IV

With the name of the deceased being spelled out when the stone is inverted, as:

DI
NO
CON
SVO
DIC
O
ON

(7) A further two stones have been discovered further west (see below).

As the mountains begin closing in the route has further Bronze Age burial cairns along its path, which at times meets with the modern track. Keeping a ready eye on the newer route, one can also occasionally spot narrow rut marks in the stones, which must be from wheeled vehicles travelling along the route at some point – perhaps evidence from the short period of time the coaches preferred the Tal y Cafn crossing for mountain pass route to Bangor.

The Roman way continues to be clearly visible, with two parallel linear marks running through the narrowing pass. As the line of pylons heads westward there is a famous cairn to the south of the track, near where the Bronze Age stone guardians of the pass straddle the way ahead – for this is the Bwlch y Ddeufaen, the Pass of the Two Stones. The burial cairn is Barclodiad y Gawres – The Giantess' Apronful (SH716716), which has a relationship in folklore with the standing stones.

Along this stretch of road, visible to the careful observer are linear markings in stones. Tokens of its use during the coaching era?

The tale runs that two giants from the east were making their way along the road to go to live in Anglesey, the giantess carrying stones in her apron, and the giant with two large stones for the door. Anglesey does not become visible until the west side of the pass. The giants met a cobbler coming in the opposite direction with shoes tied around his neck; when the giants enquired how much further the Isle was and disclosed their intention to reside there, the cunning cobbler exclaimed that Anglesey was still some way off and that all the shoes around his neck were ones he had worn out on the journey thus far. Instantly discouraged, both giant and giantess discharged their respective cumbersome loads, creating the cairn and stones that are seen today.

Near the cairn is a large prone stone, which one could easily

The Pass of the Two Stones – prehistoric and Roman routes converge on the easiest way through the mountains; the Roman road can be seen as a gorse-less line to the left of the track in the distance.

The course of the Roman road westwards to Aber.

imagine as once having been erect. The first of the main stones is soon on the left. Also of interest, and easily overlooked, are many smaller stones hidden in the grass radiating outwards to the east. These can be carefully investigated by gentle prodding with the feet – gentle so as not to damage them, and also because they constitute a tripping hazard since they are disguised amongst the taller and softer grass.

The second stone is visible on the right further up on a ridge, with at least one further standing stone in the ensemble. To the left is a ditch (possibly a quarry) or hollow way that has cut deeply across a cairn; on reaching the neck of the pass, Anglesey and Puffin Island are visible. The modern track concurs with the Roman route, but soon swings to the south leaving a very long section of Roman agger across the landscape towards Llanfairfechan. Further prehistoric burials are dotted to the south of the course of the road.

Where the Roman route crosses the line of pylons, two separate phases of Roman road become possible, though they both angle progressively north-westwards. Between these two pylons is an incised stone. A possible interpretation is that is was an arrow sharpening stone due to the nature of the rubbings in its surface, but recent opinion is that it is not typical of prehistoric polissoirs as the incisions are not broad and smooth enough. It is doubtful that any sagittari (archers) in the Roman army would have paused to sharpen arrows in such a remote place. Other possibilities remain: it might have been used by one of two other invading forces. Colonel Twistleton's advance in the Civil War utilised this same route from the Tal y Cafn ferry; assuming the Roman route was usable in the seventeenth century, then King Edward I's forces might also have taken the same inland route some three and a half centuries beforehand.

As has been shown, this stretch of road from Rowen is without equal in terms of the interpretable remains of different periods, with a rich profusion of prehistoric remains around many miles of clear stretches of hollow ways, ridges and linear features relating to the Roman(ised) route. Hereafter, unless explicitly mentioned any reference to the Roman road is in terms of just its course; nothing is interpretable on the ground.

The route onward to Segontium, having come down from the uplands near Abergwyngregyn, continues along a south-west course, with a few variations along the way. Two proposed routes approach Caernarfon at the end of the road from Canovium. One stretches from below Tal y Bont and Llandegai on an axis fairly consistent with a north-east approach; the other 'dog legs' by way of the north end of Llyn Padarn. A third apparently unconnected route traverses the way from Bangor to Caernarfon. Starting at Port Penrhyn, soon cutting across the A5122 heading south-west, this Roman line traverses with characteristic straightness the modern A5 and B4547. Further south the B4366 is intersected near Bethel, followed by a crossing of the Afon Cadant, finally cutting across the A4086 on the approach to Segontium's north-eastern side. The Llyn Padarn route from Canovium runs parallel to the Penrhyn–Caernarfon route, but somewhat inland.

This 'dog leg' alternative route to Segontium from the Bangor area takes a line west of the river flowing from Llyn Ogwen, curving south where yet another milestone has been found at Ty Coch, this time to Marcus Aurelius (Caracalla) and dating from 212–17 AD. The road bears south-west and south-south-west, arriving at a point north-east of the top of Llyn Padarn at Cae'r Bythod where another milestone contemporary with Trajan was found, dating from 249–51 AD. Not far from all these variations in route is situated the ancient British hill fort of Dinas Dinorwig (SH549653).

Between Bangor and Caernarfon the way had become more difficult by the time of Giraldus Cambrensis; traversing in the opposite direction, having left Caernarfon, "Our road led us to a valley, where the going was hard, with many steep climbs up and down. We dismounted from our horses and proceeded on foot... We walked the whole length of the valley, and we were very tired by the time we reached the farther end. The Archbishop sat himself down on an oak-tree... for he needed to rest and recover his breath." (8) This valley is said to have been Nant y Garth near Port Dinorwic (not to be confused with the Nant y Garth nearer Ruthin), and it now forms part of the driving test route from Caernarfon according to the Driving Standards Agency.

A Trajanic milestone from the Canovium to Segontium road; picture taken by the author, used courtesy of the Segontium Museum.

Segontium to Nefyn

Segontium at Caernarfon was another fortress begun by Agricola during the same campaign in which he founded the outpost at Canovium. Segontium served as the principal North Wales base from the end of the first century AD until the end of the fourth. There is no other precedent in Wales for such longevity of use.

Infantry auxiliary units were based here, totalling about 1,000 men; as at Canovium a bath house was constructed, but atypically it was situated within the fort's defences. Roman religion was also well represented, with an altar to Minerva and a Mithraeum – a temple dedicated to the Persian god Mithras. The stone used to construct the fort in the first part of the third century AD

Map 4

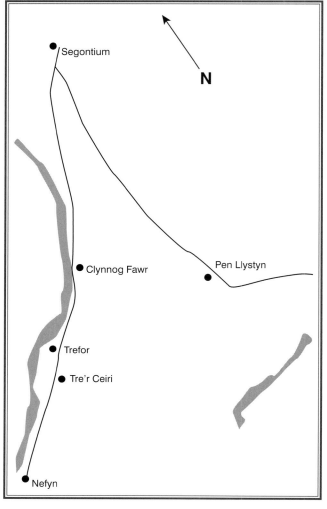

was later reused in the construction of Caernarfon Castle, a thousand years after it was initially set in place by Wales' first occupying invader. An advantage of which the later King Edward would have approved is the possibility of access to the sea and river not far from the fortress.

Significantly, Segontium has a tie-in with early mediaeval history and mythology. In the Mabinogion – a collection of early Welsh mediaeval tales – it is "Caer Aber Seiont" in "The Dream of Macsen Wledig". In this tale one of Segontium's late commanders is mentioned. Historical figure of Macsen Wledig was Magnus Maxiumus, a Spanish general who is reputed to have fought off raids in the North West from the Picts and the Irish. Macsen Wledig/Magnus Maxiumus will appear later in this chapter in relation to the Roman road known as the Sarn Helen.

Macsen Wledig is also important since later Welsh dynasties often attempt to trace their lineage to him: "The emperor Maximus impressed himself very strongly upon native Welsh tradition in two capacities: first, as the leader who deprived Britain of her fighting men and, secondly, as the ancestor from whom several of the early Welsh ruling dynasties claimed descent. The earliest instance of this claim appears on the ninth-century Valle Crucis pillar, the inscription on which traces the descent of the kings of Powys…" (9)

The route for crossing the neck of the Lleyn Peninsula leaves from the southern side of the fortress at Caernarfon. After a short distance the A4085 is crossed, and the road converges with the A487 as it leads south across the Afon Seiont through Bontnewydd to Gadlys, east of Llanwnda. Gadlys is an obvious small hill and would have served the Roman engineers' sighting methods well for travelling onward to Pen Llystyn, or departing south-west in the direction of Nefyn. Crossing the line of the A487, the A499 and the Afon Carrog, the route proceeds on the west side of the A499; the routes conjoin for around five miles.

At Clynnog Fawr the Roman road diverges from the modern one towards Trefor, where Waddelove has postulated a possible military site. Beyond Trefor the route becomes unclear for a short distance, but then leads steeply uphill, passing between the westernmost pair of the three towering mountains of the Rivals (a corruption of the Welsh "Yr Eifl"). It emerges on the west side of Yr Eifl via the pass of that name. Approaching Nefyn the route crosses the B4417 before the line is lost east of the junction with the A497, near an uncertain destination at Nefyn. It must be borne in mind that the Lleyn is on par with Anglesey for concentrations of Neolithic, Bronze Age and Iron age sites, which must be an indication of reasonable native populations at the time. The principal hillfort on the route is Tre'r Ceiri (SH373446), a lofty town once home to at least one hundred and fifty hut circles within well-preserved ramparts. It was in use several centuries before the Roman invasion, and habitation continued throughout much of the Roman occupation until the fourth century.

Segontium to Tomen y Mur via Pen Llystyn

Leaving Segontium near the river Seiont from the south-east side at a steep south-west angle, the Roman route soon joins the A487. Whereas the contemporary route then diverges considerably while keeping a largely southward direction, the Romans kept their route in a stereotypical straight line for several miles, crossing the Afon Gwyrfai at Bontnewydd, past the east side of Penygroes, to Llanllyfni and then onward to join the A487 for half a mile before the later route angles south-west of the site of the Roman fort of Pen Llystyn.

Leaving the site of Pen Llystyn fort from the south, the Roman route then bypasses the elbow of the A487, projecting in a definite line and converging with the modern road north-east of Dolbenmaen. The Afon Dwyfor is crossed as both routes, ancient and contemporary, proceed south-east. Having passed the Afon Cedron the Roman route departs along the direction indicated by its preceding stretch, cutting across the A497 west of what is now Porthmadog. The precise line across the mouth of the Glaslyn estuary is uncertain, but Waddelove postulates the possibility that Madock's 'cob' across the Glaslyn may follow the Roman line. Without an embankment to utilise in crossing, the Romans would have had to reckon on tides and weather for onward travel eastwards, akin to the drovers' cutting south-east over a thousand years later.

The route picks up again consistent with the eastbound line of the A487 towards Penrhyndeudraeth, leaving the modern route as that line angles north-east via a junction to the A4084. The A487 and the Roman road run loosely parallel to each other for a mile, after which the Roman line turns south-east. It crosses the Dwyryd and then runs eastward, cutting the A496 and the Afon Prysor near Ivy Bridge, maintaining an eastward flow and intersecting the A470.

Dolgellau to Tomen y Mur

Dolgellau is postulated as a possible Roman fort site; being at the western junction of at least three, maybe four routes there would have been a necessity for Roman fort in that area. Some of the modern street layout (largely centred upon Smithfield Street) is suggestive of the typical playing-card shape of a fort; Smithfield Street could form a Via Principalis of sorts, north-east from Eldom Square. The Roman road north and south from Dolgellau is specifically known as part of the Sarn Helen, from Carmarthen Moridunum to Canovium; more correctly it should be Sarn Elen (see discussion below). The term is sometimes used interchangeably with Roman roads in other areas; for some, "Sarn Helen" is a blanket term for all Roman roads.

Much confusion surrounds the who and what of both "Sarn" and "Helen"; as Davies noted, "In this connection a few words may also be said about the place name Sarn, which is usually supposed to refer to ancient roads, and in some instances to Roman roads, as for example, Sarn Elen (incorrectly Helen) in Caernarvonshire and Merionethshire, and which occurs as least six times in this county. There can be little doubt that originally the name Sarn had reference to a causeway in a river, stream, or bog-land. Later it came to be regarded as signifying a paved road. Camden in the sixteenth century states that the 'Britains' called 'the high military road paved with stone' 'near the

Map 5

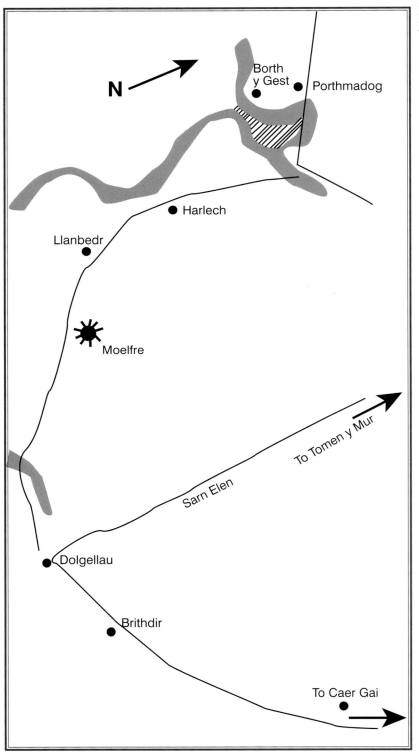

N

Borth
y Gest

Porthmadog

Harlech

Llanbedr

Moelfre

To Tomen y Mur

Sarn Elen

Dolgellau

Brithdir

To Caer Gai

little village of Festiniog' 'Sarn Elen' 'whence,' he adds, 'we may reasonably suppose it the work of Helena; the mother of Constantine.'" (10)

The lady in question could be linked with Macsen Wledig, who married Elen Lluyddog. Outliving him, she went on to many notable achievements, including efforts pertaining to the roads. In that case she is better referred to as Elen, not Helen. Some may dismiss this as pedantry, but the confusion as to which person is being referred to ought to be addressed. Bromwich records that Elen "…appears to have been a character of early Welsh mythology who was particularly associated with the Roman roads in Wales (hence her epithet Lluyddog, 'of the Hosts'). The Roman roads are known to this day as Sarn(au) Helen. But at an early stage, as Ifor Williams showed in 1927 (in his introduction to Breudwyt Maxen), her identity became confused with that of the Roman St Helena, mother of Constantine the Great, who, according to a legend which goes back to the fourth century, had made a pilgrimage to Jerusalem and discovered the true Cross." (11)

The exact known start to the Sarn Elen route is uncertain, but crossings of both the earlier part of the Afon Mawddach and later the Afon Eden would have been required as the route weaves around the existing A470. A clearer route then becomes identifiable from SH723293, staying east of the A470 as it winds its way around the green dome-like hill with the Craig y Penmaen, and then using the ridge as a clear means of keeping the landscape and way ahead visible. Further along the course there is another easily identifiable stretch of Roman road earthworks near Tomen y Mur, and also remains of Roman kilns just to the east at SH726319. In terms of the obvious good sense of having industrial and manufacturing centres in close proximity to supply and communications routes, this serves as a good example. The route loses its clarity at SH723338.

As the route heads towards Tomen y Mur there are the remains of a mansio (SH707388) – a Roman coaching inn or staging post on the south-east approach to the fort.

The agger of the Roman road at 0 south from Tomen y Mur; earthworks right to left, slightly marked to assist locating the line.

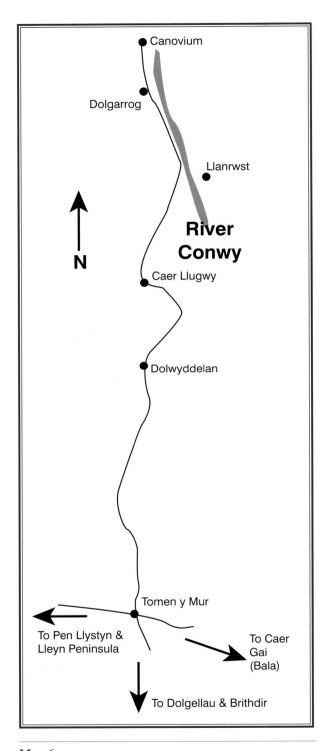

Map 6

Tomen y Mur to Canovium via Caer Llugwy

The proposed route here exits from the north-western end of the Roman rectangle, with a fork in the direction of Pen Llystyn. Continuing on course for Caer Llugwy the way heads north-east, passing across the A470 and making a decisive swing north-west across the A496 and Afon Cynfal at Pont Rhiw Felen. Crossing the Afon Teigl shortly thereafter, the route stays on the eastern side of the larger Afon Goedol and west of the Bowydd as the A496 curves to the west approaching Blaenau Ffestiniog. Unsurprisingly given the degree of later industrialisation, throughout this area the slate tips and quarries obliterate anything and everything under them. North of Blaenau Ffestiniog Waddelove's route takes a more westerly course than the modern A470, keeping to the west of Roman Bridge train station not far from Dolwyddelan Castle (the bridge being named after an older crossing attributed to the Romans).

The siting of a castle here lends a commanding view of the valley. Dolwyddelan is constructed upon the east side of a ridge from which point it dominates the Lledr valley as well as the road from the Conwy valley to Ardudwy. The castle was probably built under the auspices of Llywelyn ab Iorwerth around 1210, with later work likely to have been done by Edward I. The tower as it can be seen today was comprehensively restored in the mid-nineteenth century.

The continuation of Waddelove's route proceeds in a north-easterly line across Afon Ystumiau before a short swing to the north, joining the upper stretch of the traditional route to enter the camp at Caer Llugwy on the south-east side.

The alternative route past Blaenau Ffestiniog is lost under the slate works, but

The modern minor road a short distance north-west of Sarn Elen from Tomen Y Mur, before it intersects the B4391.

a long straight road emerges into the enclosing Cwm Penamner from SH733493, passing through a narrow exit below Dolwyddelan. The crossing of the Lledr takes the road further, with an uncertain link to the north-east. Sarn Elen picks up on the map at SH756543 for a short while, and again north of Rhiwddolion (SH773561), avoiding a difficult climb over Mynydd Cribau by taking a curvilinear way around the south of the Afon Llugwy to the fort. (12)

For the northward march to Canovium, the way ahead lies north-westward taking the route which the drovers later used. This provides the easiest passage to the west of the Conwy valley near Llanrwst. A fording of the Llugwy would be required, and then an ascent towards Llyn Sarnau, a place name suggestive of old tracks in the area. Passing over the east shoulder of Mynydd Bwlchyrhaearn the route emerges into the river valley to the north-west of Llanrwst with its important later bridge crossing. The Roman road remains on or slightly below the route of the B5106; the local geography means there is not a lot of space for variation for much of the riverside journey. North-north-west from Trefriw is Trefriw Wells spa – a chalybeate water source said to have been first discovered and utilised by the Twentieth Legion who were based in Chester for substantial periods. The spring found new life from 1833 onwards into the Victorian heyday of spa visits.

Earlier use of the west of the Conwy valley is shown by the presence of a Neolithic burial chamber, Porth Llwyd, situated just north of Dolgarrog (SH770678). Located close to the banks of Afon Porth, the site was very badly damaged in 1925 in a disaster. The failure of the upper Llyn Eigiau reservoir dam had a knock-on effect for the Coety reservoir beneath; Dolgarrog was swamped in the resulting flood, which destroyed buildings and took sixteen lives. The tomb of Porth Llwyd was on the very edge of the torrent. The remaining stones are said to form part of a field boundary; the capstone, which originally sat on top of the monument and which was the largest stone, now lies on its edge. (13)

The Roman road proceeds just east of Dolgarrog, heading north and crossings- the rivers Dulyn and Roe, eventually entering the fortress at Canovium on its south-western side.

St Asaph (Varis) to Corwen (Penrhos)

From the junction of the Roman east–west corridor, a further route departs southward following the west side of the Vale of Clwyd. The route keeps loosely to the course of the A525 in the direction of Trefant, staying to the east of Denbigh and on to Llanrhaeadr. It then skims the south-west of Rhewl and Ruthin (where there is the remains of a fort), crossing the A494 and departing towards the A525 at Llanfair Dyffryn Clwyd before curving to the south-west near Llanelidan close to the course of the B5429. The route descends in a line almost equidistant between the joining of the A5104 and A494 north from the native fort of Caer Drewyn. Just north-west of Corwen at Clawdd Poncen it joins the projected route from Chester. Staying west of the Dee, it makes its only river crossing at the Alwen east of Druid, finally arriving at the fort at Penrhos (SJ044426).

Deva to Dolgellau

This projected route from Deva is not picked up until some way south-west of Chester, at Ffridd (also Frith) along the line of a minor road in parallel with the A525 (SJ272543). It then follows the route of the A5104 at Llandegla and the suggestively-named Pen y Stryt (bearing in mind the place name link to Street – the Anglo-Saxon name for a Roman road). This track then makes its way south-west onto the high ground largely parallel with the A5104, descending east of Gwyddelwern to join the course of that modern road and converging with the route from St Asaph and Bala to the south-west.

A discovery made through aerial photography in July 2006 found a hitherto unrecognised stretch of Roman road revealed as a parch mark upon the ground, heading north-east and south-west from SJ048439. It continues in a line north-east of Four Crosses near Druid on the A5 with a river crossing near Pen y Bont. (14)

The route proceeds south-west towards Bala, staying well west of the Dee. Of relevance are more prehistoric monuments in the area. The Iron Age hillfort of Caer Euni at SJ000413 has some unusual vitrified defences whereby the stone ramparts were burnt by having wood placed over and between them, hardening and fusing the stones together. Vitrification in hillforts is much more common in Scotland and quite rare south of the Scottish Borders. The Bronze Age circles of Cefn Caer Euni (SH993410) and the standing stone of Coed y Bedo (SH966400) are also on ancient trackways. Further east in the Dee Valley a cluster of Neolithic and Bronze Age monuments indicate much pre-Roman usage as a thoroughfare. These are the Neolithic burial chamber remains at Tyn y Coed (SJ048397), Branas Uchaf (SJ012375), the Bronze Age Tyfos stone circle(SJ028388) to the north, and the destroyed stone circle of Pabell Llwyarch Hen (SH940366) nearer to Bala. Without doubt, it is certain that there were well-used routes in the area by the time the Romans arrived.

For place name evidence of the Roman route progressing south-west, one could not find much more of a giveaway than the village names of Sarnau and Cefn Ddwysarn – "sarn" of course denoting a trackway or causeway. Above the north tip of Lake Bala the route arrives at the fort of Llanfor, with the track continuing south-westerly east of the A494 but west of the lake. On reaching Caer Gai, offset somewhat to the south-west tip of the lake at SH878314, the projected route to the fort at Brithdir then continues towards Dolgellau, crossing over the A494 near Rhyd Sarn, staying to the

A stretch of road south-east from the fort at Penrhos near Corwen. The elevation of the bank on the right suggests a hollow way and a route of antiquity – possibly Roman.

east and then approaching Brithdir from the east. Dolgellau with its postulated Roman fort is then a short march away to the south-west.

Tomen y Mur via Caer Gai to Newtown

This route, insofar as the geographical remit of this work covers its course, is only known in three definite stretches. Departing Tomen y Mur south-easterly, the route is clear until shortly before it meets the A4212 across Cwm Prysor east of Trawsfynydd. It is not until further south-east from Caer Gai, at the south-east tip of Lake Bala, that the way can be deciphered once more as it takes the ridge above Cwm Cynllwyd, staying north of many small tributaries of Afon Fechan and Nant y Tryfal on a course to pass the summit of Foel y Geifr to the south. The track then joins the Cwm Hirnant route from Rhos y Gwaliau on its approach to Rhiwargor (SH948262) north-west of Lake Vyrnwy. The route here was chosen by virtue of the elevation of its passage, not for the use of the reservoir for marking the way – Lake Vyrnwy was not constructed until the 1880s, for the first time flooding a North Wales valley and village to supply Merseyside with water (this happened again 80 years later in the creation of Llyn Celyn north of Bala). East of Lake Vyrnwy the course of the route is lost, being found again north-west from Llanfihangel yng Ngwynfa. It heads south and intersecting the A4393 and then angles south-westwards parallel to the B4382 for a short stretch, crossing the Afon Efyrnwy and shortly thereafter the Afon Banwy. It is not picked up again until well south of the A458, north-west of Llanllugan. One may project a crossing of the modern route in the Llanerfyl and Four Crosses area.

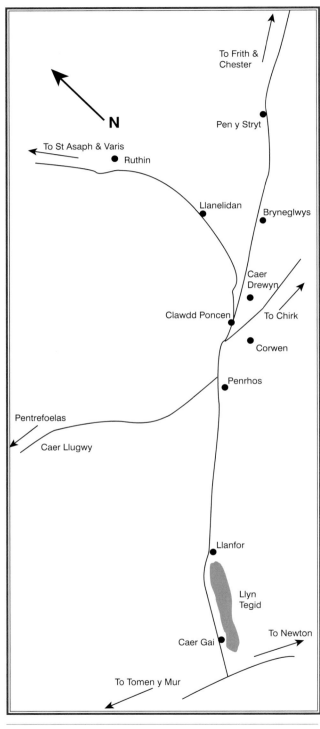

Map 7

Lleyn Peninsula to Dolgellau

This route is the proposal of Edmund Waddelove; given the array of Neolithic tombs and Bronze Age features en route (see Fonlief Hir in Chapter Two), and the almost identical use of the route until the drovers (even if the Romans did not invest their time and effort into bringing the way into line with their methods), it remains a credible passage from the north-west. Leaving southbound from the crossing of the Glaslyn estuary and Traeth Mawr, the proposed Roman way soon navigates the Afon Dwyryd and Traeth Bach just east of Portmeirion. A route about a third of mile further east is picked up on the southern shore and soon cuts the A496, remaining to the east of the modern route. It crosses the train track north of Harlech Castle and passes King Edward's fortification close by on the east. It rejoins the modern route at Llanfair, continuing south-east along Sarn Hir north of Llanbedr.

The route is now heading into terrain used later by the drovers from Harlech and the Lleyn, and by the London to Harlech coach. Indication that these travellers were following an earlier route is given weight by an extensive settlement in the fields east of the flattened Cors y Gedol burial chamber (SH603228). A variety of earthworks reveal a succession of dwellings and farming from the first millennium BC, through the Roman period and up to the sixteenth century at least, with subsequent farmers utilising earlier structures in many places. This can make for difficult interpretation when one takes into account the growth of gorse and bracken. (15)

The Roman route across the Rhinogs to Dolgellau proposed by Waddelove, a short way past the settlements and fields used for over 2,500 years from prehistory to the sixteenth century.

One of the standing stones near the proposed Roman route over the Rhinogs; Pont Scethin out of sight bottom left, and the postulated Roman way following a modern track marked with lines.

The Roman route then angles towards a crossing of the Afon Ysgethin, where there is now Pont Scethin, having skirted around the huge dome of Moelfre to the north-east. Before the bridge are two standing stones south of the track aligned with Y Llethr, the tallest part of the Rhinogs. The route then follows the steep ascent angling across the contours of Braich, past the memorial to Janet Haigh erected by her son, a Bishop of Winchester paying homage to his mother's use of this way to Dolgellau into advanced old age. Having heeded the encouraging salution of "Courage Traveller" and traversed uphill, the route descends to Pont Hirgwm, crossing Bontddu and the A496 from the north-west. The track then crosses the Mawddach, with the continuation of the route over the A493 eastwards to Dolgellau, staying south of the A493, the A470 and the Afon Wnion.

Segontium to Caer Llugwy via Llanberis Pass

Leaving Segontium from the south-east, the Roman route follows the A4085 for just over a quarter of a mile, after which it maintains its linear progression over the Afon Seiont and crosses the A4085 further east. Swinging around to a more direct easterly route through the pass of Bwlch y Groes, the route then turns south-east to descend on the south-west of Llanberis, meeting the A4086 on the neck of land between lakes Padarn and Peris.

The significance of guarding this route was demonstrated in the early thirteenth century, when Llywelyn ab Iorwerth, prince of the kingdom of Gwynedd, had Dolbadarn Castle constructed. Like other Welsh castles it soon fell into abandonment after King Edward completed his suppression of Wales. A curious structure of stones at Parc Bach (SH585598), on top of a wooded knoll near the castle, contains a little-known megalithic tomb-like structure. Earlier use of a route through this area is hinted at by the place name of 'Pont y Gromlech' as the route continues through the Pass of Llanberis. Its exact line is not clear, though the opportunity for diversion away from passable territory is minimal.

The course continues to reach the camp at Pen-y-Gwryd, through the final climb and swing to the north-east at Bwlch y Gwyddel (the Irish connection appearing once more in the place name). The Roman camp still straddles the A4086 and A498 with defences some two millennia after the Romans guarded the pass. World War II pillboxes guard a place as strategically important today in the event of a land invasion as it was for the Romans. Leaving the site of the camp to the north-east in a line north and parallel to the A4086, the route approaches Capel Curig from the south-west, where the Roman road is believed to be close to the line of the A5 until it meets the road north from Caer Llugwy to Canovium with the last crossing of the Afon Llugwy.

Caer Llugwy to Bangor via Nant Ffrancon

Once again the suggestion of Waddelove, the Roman road would exit from the north-west corner of the fort in the meadow south of the Llugwy river, crossing the river and following the A5 very closely until Capel Curig. Continuing straight across at the current crossroads, the Llugwy is crossed once more whereupon the road follows a route tight to the base of the crags. The later road from the coaching era swings much wider and closer to the river at this point. Having worked around the outcrops, the Roman route and coach route rejoin for some distance, crossing the Afon Denau (which feeds into Lake Ogwen) and then taking the current line of the A5 adjacent to the greater length of the lake.

The route departs from the modern road (built by Telford) close to the Idwal Cottage youth hostel, taking a wider arc to the west side of the glacial coombe of Nant Ffrancon. It then descends steeply, cutting out the curve of the existing lane, and proceeds to closely weave around this modern tarmac-covered surface until the present-day route departs north-easterly to rejoin the A5. The Roman route

The Pass of Llanberis at Pont y Gromlech before 1925; note the cart just before the bridge. Postcard in author's collection, copyright holder and publisher not identifiable.

The modern road bisecting the earthworks of the Roman fort at Pen-y-Gwryd, most clearly visible on the right-hand side; marks added to help spot the linear earthworks.

can then be extrapolated through the Penrhyn Slate Quarries, taking a course west of Bethesda and the Afon Ogwen through Llandegai and Penrhyn Park.

Rhyn Park (Chirk) to Caer Llugwy

Tracing the route right back to the later border with England, this is a projected road for reaching the heart of Snowdonia from the east. (16) Departing Rhyn Park by the north-west corner then closely following the course of the current A5 from its angle towards the Vale of Llangollen, the route passes Froncysyllte. The proposed Roman road then departs from the line of the A5 west of Llangollen, just south of the Horseshoe Falls, where a fording of the River Dee is probable. This takes the route on to the north bank of the Dee, removing the need for further river crossings as it meanders through the valley.

This location was significant both before and after the Romans as a place to watch movement through the area around. The evocative hill of Dinas Bran was home to an Iron Age community long before the Welsh lords of Powys Fadog constructed their stunning thirteenth-century castle upon the summit as testimony to their prestige, wealth and power. The hill is suggested as one of the burial places of The Holy Grail.

The route bypasses the river's swings through the valley by taking understandable cuts around their curves, or across the neck of land. The current A494 is intersected as the route passes north of the confluence between the Dee and the Alwen. At this point several routes meet – the Roman road crosses a possible line from Chester weaving around the line of the A5104 (as per the proposed prehistoric track, with the British defended settlement of Caer Drewyn looking over the meeting of the rivers and ways). This line would continue towards Bala and Caer Gai. A further route comes from the Chester–Canovium road, departing at St Asaph and continuing past Ruthin (see above).

Following Telford's modern road but with some variation from the drovers' route, Waddelove continues the westward and progressively northward track across the open moorland to Cerrigydrudion. The Afon Alwen is crossed at Pont Melin-Rug, with a characteristically straight section of the A5 superimposed upon the Roman course south of the river at Druid. Where the modern road diverges to the north-west the Roman route departs at an even steeper angle, crossing the Afon Ceirw at Pont Rhyd-llefrith, remaining south of the A5 below Dinmael and then heading north-west again, keeping to the north-east side of the tarmac surface and river. The way curves to the north, cutting below a British fort by the name of Caer Caradoc (one of many throughout Wales recalling the legendary resistance of Caradoc/Caratacus against the Romans). Another prehistoric marker stands at the east end of Cerrigydrudion; the village's name means "The Stones of the Druid". To the right of the A5 a Bronze Age barrow can still be seen as a shallow depleted earthwork; as is often the case, the Romans again seem to be following earlier routes which have remained the best paths for millennia.

Continuing westwards, the Roman route runs nearly parallel to Telford's modern road, but then just east of the A543 it angles north-west once more, staying to the north of Pentrefoelas across the open moors before descending to Betws y Coed. Further prehistoric remains in this area attest to earlier routes: there are the remains of the Neolithic Cotwsold-Severn tomb at Capel Garmon (SH818543), and closer to the proposed Roman route stand the multiple stone rows of Hafod y Garreg and Hafod y Dre. The rock of Carreg Lleon is suggestive too since its name means "the Rock of the Legion".

The descent to the crossing of the Conwy takes a line north-east of Waterloo Bridge, fording the strategic frontier of the Conwy below the present train station. The ancient way cuts across the A5 through the town centre, hugging the south side of the road closely until the modern route arcs northward; a further two intersections of the road occur in quick succession, the first just west of the Swallow Falls and the second to the south side of the A5 bridge below The Ugly House (Ty Hyll), as the road nears its intended destination at the fort of Caer Llugwy on the south side of the river.

Anglesey

As previously noted, the apparent dearth of Roman roads on Anglesey seemed to be a puzzle, but there do exist several stretches of route which may be attributed to the Romans. In keeping with every other major route on the isle, the Roman ways are aimed at traversing the land to arrive at Holyhead.

The eastern route is much more fragmented and piecemeal in its projection. Having crossed the Menai Strait, landing perhaps west of Ynys Gaint, the road heads north towards Plas Cadnant, intersecting the A5025 just west of a standing stone and then veering north-west on a course in line with a track next to Bryn-eryr. After this point the way is unclear, but it is likely that it aims toward Rhoscefnhir, becoming more apparent west of Pentraeth adjacent to a Bronze Age barrow. Briefly the road converges with the B5109 before departing cross-country again next to the menhir at Llanddyfnan. An even more vague curvilinear arc is projected, with a stretch of straight track being picked up at Sarnfadog (SH420812), which if extrapolated westwards would point to Holyhead.

The western route is much more definite in most of its projection, with some variations in its route. The starting point would appear to be a landing place across from Segontium just below Talgwynedd, SH464637. From here a jagged course along the same basic axis heads through Dwyran crossing Afon Braint to join the B4421 south-west of the important historic church at Llangaffo (one of many on Anglesey). The church is home to an early seventh century gravestone along with others from the ninth to twelfth centuries, and there is a wheeled cross fragment inside and a shaft outside the building thought to be contemporary with the fine specimen at Penmon on the island's eastern

The historic bridge into Aberffraw dated 1731, now for unmotorised traffic only; a hugely important settlement in the mediaeval period, was there also a Roman presence at Aberffraw?

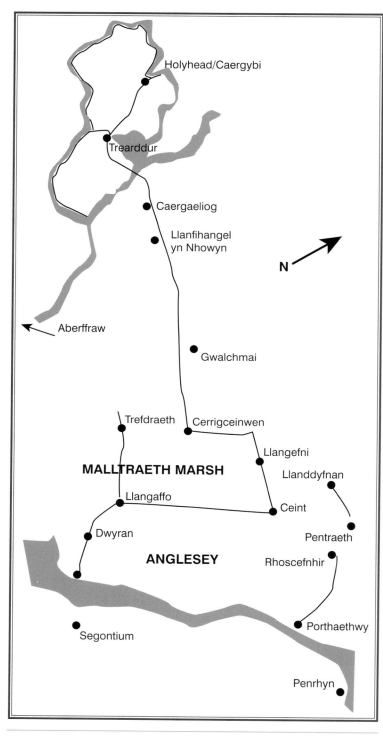

Map 8

tip. The site was home to a very early mediaeval monastery, retaining its significance from the Roman era; the more modern church is adjacent to the long straight lane following the ridgeway.

Before the church, the road passes to the west of an intense area of prehistoric activity, of obvious significance for the Romans. The tallest standing stones in Wales, thought by antiquarian romantics to once have been part of a stone circle, burial chambers and barrows around Brynsiencyn, the henge-cum-defended Iron Ige settlement of Castell Bryn Gwyn, and the Romano-British settlement of Caer Leb – all provide evidence of extensive life in these parts before the Romans.

Just south-west from Llangaffo, another lane points north-westwards apparently terminating 'nowhere'. This would have been one of the crossings of the Malltraeth Marsh and Afon Cefni, the other end of which is picked up again north-east of Malltraeth at SH419696, following the lane to Trefdraeth and Bethel. This particular track is lost from this point on, though one may project a link to the longer route (below) joining at Cerrigceinwen along the B4422, or even more speculatively, it may continue on course to the possible Roman fort at Aberffraw.

Returning to Llangaffo, the wider circumnavigation of the Malltreath Marsh involves a rectilinear detour via Llangefni. After a brief arc above St Caffo's church the Roman road follows the ridge fairly consistently with the B4419. The line of the A5 is intersected and a fording of a tributary of the Afon Ceint, itself a tributary of the Cefni, takes place at Rhyd-yr-arian. The road curves towards Ceint, joining the course of the pre-A5 coach road with a minor loop on its south side, all the way through Llangefni along the B5420. Having avoided the broad swathe of marsh, the Roman way turns south-west through Rhostrehwfa along the course of the B4422, and then cuts west through Cerrigceinwen.

From Tyddyn Sadler there are a couple of possible variations in route, both converging beneath Gwalchmai. The road cuts across country once more, staying beneath the course of the A5, south of Bryngwran and north of Llanfihangel yn Nhowyn. A field here marked as Cae Elen could be linking in with the tradition of Elen of the Roads (see above). The route joins the road converging with Caergeiliog, and until the junction at Valley it runs concurrent with the course of the A5 and then turns south-west with the B4545 to cross at the site of Four Mile Bridge. Iron Age hut circles (the Cytiau'r Gwyddelod) stand on a peninsula north of this crossing. The curving road to Trearddur is followed, at which point the Roman route diverges to take the road past the multi-phase burial chambers of Trefignath and the twisted standing stone of Ty Mawr (now being developed into a retail park as the sprawl of the town continues), on course to approach Caergybi, the fort at Holyhead.

CHAPTER 4

Roads and Trackways of Pilgrimage

At first the idea of pilgrim roads and trackways may appear something of a misnomer. People on spiritual quests do not construct roads. However, if a particular destination is converged on over a long time by travellers engaged upon pilgrimage, then to speak of the way there as a pilgrim road is justifiable. North Wales is particularly rich in holy places where people would come on pilgrimage, for a variety of reasons – either for local pilgrimages from surrounding dwellings and parishes, or for others, from much further afield. Pilgrimage continues today albeit by different means of transport; historically it was something that was engaged in on quite a scale if the sources and assumptions are true.

Akin to prehistoric trackways, pilgrim roads are not so much about the surface of the way taken, but about the monuments and features along the way. Monasteries, churches, chapels, wayside crosses and holy wells are places that would have formed the pilgrims' route. One of the difficulties of dealing with holy places in Wales was succinctly articulated thus: "The problem with writing about Wales in a book on sacred Britain is that virtually the whole of Wales seems sacred. Look at place-names for example. Any place which begins with the ubiquitous Llan signifies a special, usually holy, enclosure. Visit such a place and you will probably find a church of great antiquity, beside a flowing stream or well. Wales in its very fabric is sacred."(1)

Glancing through an atlas or map of Wales, these places prefixed by 'Llan' usually indicate some site of early Christian importance, which based on indicative and often anecdotal evidence are 'carry overs' from pre-Christian sacred sites. Find a circular churchyard, some large yew trees, maybe even a standing stone or two incorporated into the church, the churchyard wall or even among the relatively more modern gravestones, and one can infer a continuation of veneration at the site. Churches on mounds, or at the highest part of the surrounding community, may be well also be

Ynys Enlli – (Bardsey Island), destination for a tradition of pilgrimage routes encompassing the entire Lleyn Peninsula.

upon prehistoric sites. Whether or not these pre-Christian sites have been translated into the new religion by adoption into an identifiably Christ centred cult is not essential to them being a sacred site. A site set apart (set-apart being the definition of sacred) for venerating, meeting or appeasing something otherworldy. As seen above, the number of ancient sites which have already been noted shows a sacred, interconnected landscape, with threads woven with each generation.

Visits to sacred places did not start with Christianity: "There were pilgrims in what is now England not only before there were Englishmen, but before there were Christians. The idea of journeying to a sacred place in search of enlightenment or cure was familiar to the Romans and to the peoples they incorporated into their empire…" (2) The same is true for Wales. There were major ritual sites where items were deposited in honour of the local deity, great or small. One pre-Roman shrine in particular is at Llyn Cerrig Bach, a short distance from one of Telford's octagonal tollhouses off the A5 on Anglesey (SH306765). This lake was home to ritual deposits of votive offerings including swords, chariot wheels and chains, with the metalwork dating from between 200 BC and 60 AD – when the Roman conquest once and for all silenced any resistance from the Isle.

With the spread of Christianity between 300 and 500 AD, courtesy of movement across the Roman empire, the new faith took hold. Missionary efforts from Gaul and Ireland began to establish centres for sending out yet more missionaries. Early monasteries sprang up as a wealth of new saints created communities and forged links between them across the region. As these saints performed miracles both credible and not so credible (with fabulous legends formed around many of them), and as they lived and died, places and remains which people desired to visit were established, incrementing as the centuries progressed.

Early centres known as 'clasau' (singular, 'clas'), which were monasteries-cum-colleges, existed at Anelog (Lleyn), Bangor, Bardsey, Beddgelert, Clynnog, Penmachno and Penmon. Among other early monastic sites were Abergele, St Asaph, Llangollen (Valle Crucis) and Meifod. Bangor-is-y-Coed (also known as Bangor on Dee near the English border) was founded around 560 by Saint Dunod, but was destroyed following the Battle of Chester in 616 after the defeat of the Welsh by Aethelfrith. Twelve hundred monks were said to have been slaughtered by Aethelfrith's forces, the monks having prayed against them and incurred the victor's wrath.

The marked line has been changed and does not make sense. Survivors from this are believed to have retreated to the safety of distant Bardsey, taking some of the casualties with them, adding to the numbers of monastics already buried there. (3)

The Synod of Whitby in 664 changed the face of the now native Christian spirituality which had evolved in isolation from Roman influence, and the Roman Church became the dominant form. Four hundred years later the Norman Conquest brought French castles and French churches to the English and the Welsh borders, with cultural assimilation seeping through with the religious orders from France. The Savignac Order, soon to merge with the Cistercians in 1147, proved more acceptable to the Welsh than the Benedictines. Basingwerk in Flintshire, founded by the Cistercians in 1131, absorbed Savignac monks into the existing monastery. Used by Giraldus Cambrensis in 1188, Basingwerk was later affected by the Dissolution in 1536. Strata Marcella near Welshpool served as the mother establishment for the Savignacs, with the later Valle Crucis (1201) north of the Dee near Llangollen as a daughter abbey along with Basingwerk. Valle Crucis took its name from the tall Mercian early ninth century cross shaft, Eliseg's Pillar, which is linked by a politically postulated genealogical inscription to Macsen Wledig (see Roman roads and Sarn Elen), and even Vortigern.

In the 1200s, native monastic orders merged with the Augustinians, founded by St Augustine of Hippo who died around 430 AD.

This absorption affected Bardsey, Penmon and Beddgelert. However, this Augustine is not to be confused with Augustine of Canterbury, the first Archbishop sent by Pope Gregory the Great in 595 to bring the British into the Roman fold and deal with heresies. To make matters even more potentially confounding, Augustine of Canterbury was a Benedectine prior, not an Augustinian, who followed the Rule of Saint Benedict from sixth century Italy. At the same time as the Welsh priories were coming under Augustinian rule, the Order of the Knights Hospitaller set up their hospice at present-day Ysbyty Ifan. Aberconwy Abbey, another Cistercian site, was moved by King Edward I from the west side of the mouth of the Conwy, further up-stream to the east side of the river at Maenan.

With centuries of Roman Catholic spirituality shaping religious practices, pilgrimage gained popularity in the Middle Ages and grew with the development of the sales of indulgences and the doctrine of Purgatory. By purchasing indulgences (first offered for sale in 1095 by Pope Urban II), a certificate could be obtained confirming that the person named would have to spend less time in Purgatory, that unpleasant intermediary stage before Heaven. The fourteenth century was the heyday for pilgrimage, with North Wales possessing two particular places of patronage for pilgrims: St Winefride's at Holywell; and Bardsey Island.

In today's secularised Europe the notion of pilgrimage may seem alien and difficult to understand. Pilgrimage was important in the Middle Ages not only because of indulgences to be bought, but in order to seek healing, undertaking a literal quest into the unknown to symbolise the pilgrimage of life; pilgrimage could be undertaken on behalf of another who was unable to go themselves, or in order to accompany those for whom the journey would be difficult unaided. Significant life events may also stimulate the need for pilgrimage.

A sign in St Asaph Cathedral explains pilgrimage in the context of people pausing to view the relics of St Asaph himself: "Pilgrims would have stopped by to look at them [the relics], and to spend some time with God, often on their way to other places, such as Bardsey Island. Sometimes pilgrimage was undertaken to make amends for some wrong committed. Sometimes it was undertaken to gain holy merit. Sometimes it was the long held dream to visit these holy places. Sometimes the purpose would be to gain healing from some illness. Sometimes pilgrims would come for a great feast day, to celebrate their faith. Pilgrimage was then, as now, seen as an outward expression of an internal journey, a journey of the soul. Often in the walking from place to place, the talking to strangers met on the way, would come a clarity of vision and a renewed purpose in life."

The technical term is 'peregrination', from the Latin 'peregrinus' which originally meant someone who was simply an aimless wanderer, though it has come to mean the dedicated journey of a pilgrim. The pilgrim would also have been able to purchase souvenirs in some places, such as badges and ampullae which could be used to contain holy water from wells or oil from shrines. The badges were retained and on completion of the journey they were placed in locations where the holiness conferred by the places visited could bless fields, houses, livestock – whatever was deemed worthy of blessing. A continuation of the Iron Age practice of water veneration was to drop the badges in fords – in much the same way as people still toss coins into wells nowadays. Ampullae could also be used as a means of transferring a blessing to a locale, or could serve as a relic near an altar. There is little known evidence of these practices in Wales, and none in North Wales, though there is one nearby example in Meols on the Wirral. The others Welsh examples are in Pembrokeshire. (4) Collecting cockleshells and scallop shells as the sign of a pilgrimage were also popular with some churches still using them for baptisms, and similarly white stones were often left at poignant places en route.

A change also wrought by the coming of Norman spirituality concerned relics – items associated with, touched by, or even part of a saint which if venerated allowed the vicarious honouring of God, and possibly conferred blessings or healing to the pilgrim. In general "… the early church in Wales buried its saints, preserving and revering objects associated with them during their lifetime such as bells, books, staffs and clothing. The Norman church brought a change of emphasis, venerating the physical remains of saints and elevating their status as relics." (5)

Times were not always good for pilgrimage. The Black Death would have had a heavy impact on pilgrimage as the infrastructure of society fragmented in the face of the plague. Monarchs also had a prohibitive influence upon the practice. Henry VIII with his Catholic antagonism outlawed shrines and ordered their destruction in 1538, not to mention the dissolution of the monasteries, which impacted not only destinations such as Bardsey but also many of the places along the way. Such antipathy continued with Elizabeth I from 1558 to 1603, who held 'popish' practices in contempt. No doubt many of the frustrations articulated in the late sixteenth century concerning these heinous, superstitious beliefs were influenced by their monarch's distaste. The iconoclastic age of Cromwell and the Civil War, when so much of antiquity was destroyed, disrespected and defiled, formed a logical consummation with them, adding to the numbers of monastics already buried there.

The pilgrim routes continue in use today, although the methods of travel are very different. Places like Holywell still have pilgrims visiting year round. The routes along the coast and across country are only walked in part. Obvious developments in transport, the volume of traffic, not to mention modern medicine and a turning away from indulgences have seen to that. Today's pilgrim usually follows the routes for personal reasons – be they history, archaeology, interesting places, or indeed, as part of a spiritual journey.

Early Christian Route – Llandanwg to Chester

The first trackway to be examined is even earlier than the traditional pilgrim roads. It consists of a proposed route from St Tanwg's church, in the sand dunes at Llandanwg near Harlech, to Chester,

The churchyard at St Tanwg's near Harlech, an early Christian site from the time of St Patrick, and the start of the proposed route to Chester.

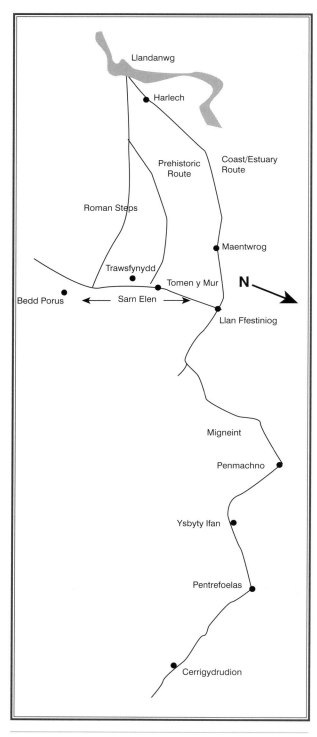

Map 1

based largely upon a chain of fifth and early sixth century memorials.

As well as providing a safer inland route that would avoid the crossing of estuaries (either the Glaslyn or the Conwy), the site at St Tanwg's could act as a port for boats from Wicklow and Kilkenny near Dunlaoghaire in Ireland, which would angle their seabound route via Barsdey Island to the Gwynedd mainland. Seven intermediary churches and sites are named on the way to Chester along this route: St Madryn at Trawsfynydd; Tomen y Mur; Ffestiniog; Penmachno; Pentrefoelas; Cerrigydrudion; and Clocaenog. It could have formed a route by which St Patrick's missionaries thrust into the mainland. The chronological distribution of memorials in Wales starts with the earliest in the west, with later memorials in the east.

By way of supporting evidence from place names, reaching into Cardigan Bay for over eleven miles is a sub-aquatic causeway upon which a good number of ships have fared ill; it is called Sarn Badrig, or Saint Patrick's Causeway, though this may be nothing more than a corruption of 'badrhywg', the Welsh word for shipwreck. It is associated with the flooded plain of Cardigan Bay and the Atlantean-like flooding which is related in tales of Cantre'r Gwaelod, this causeway anecdotally serving as one of the embankments in those stories. The line is actually a vast elongated deposition of material washed down by melt water when the glaciers departed Snowdonia in the last ice age. In appropriate tidal conditions there is nearly dry land over two and half miles out into the sea – an obvious hazard for seafarers. On the one hand it is an obstruction, but for those who know of its location, it could serve a navigational aid to a landing place for seafarers approaching an unfamiliar coastline.

Some have proposed that St Tanwg's

church (SH569282) is "The Mother Church of North Merioneth" of North Wales, based on evidence that it has been in use as a site of worship since the early fifth century derived from a stone inscribed "Ingenuus", who was a contemporary of St Patrick. A circular enclosure to the east of the church may well be mediaeval, typical of the 'llan' type of enclosure. St Tanwg's is also thought to be a mortuary chapel for the dead being taken to Bardsey. (6)

The next clue along the route is in the wilderness south-east of Trawsfynydd near the southern mountain route to Bala (curiously not recorded as an important route at any time). Not far from Llech Idris standing stone and a good stretch of the Sarn Elen is a late fifth or early sixth century grave. Bedd Porus (SH733314) is nowhere near any consecrated burial ground and is something of a puzzle. The remains there today are a fragmented copy of the original, now in a musuem. The inscription reads: "Porus lies here in the mound. He was a plain man." There are some letters missing, and debate over the meaning of 'plain man' – it could indicate that he had lost his nose to leprosy, or that he was a Christian! If this formed part of a chain of memorials along an early Christian route, it would be more direct to use the prehistoric route beginning nearby at Llanbedr and running to Trawsfynydd (as did Giraldus Cambrensis over six centuries later), rather than loop via Maentwrog to Trawsfynydd. The next three stones of importance are now within the church of Saint Tudclud at Penmachno. (7)

The way ahead takes a minor detour from the Sarn Elen, progressing northward to the site of he church at Trawsfynydd. This has a mediaeval origin but the building was restored in 1853–4 in

The crossing of the Conwy at Ysbyty Ifan, used by pilgrims and drovers for centuries on the inland route.

character with many other churches in the area. It is said that St Madryn (also Madrun) and a maid took shelter for the night at the location, each having the dream that they had to build a church here. (8)

The pilgrim route, having passed the historically lakeless landscape of Trawsfynydd and Tomen y Mur, would then go to Ffestiniog, believed to have been home to the Cantiorix stone. It is inscribed in Latin, and translates as "Cantorix lies here. He was a citizen of Venedos cousin of Maglos the magistrate". No other stone using the terms 'magistrate' and 'citizen' survives from this period in Britain. It also refers to the early form of Gwynedd – 'Venedos'.

From Ffestiniog the best route would seem to be from Pont yr Afon Gam, taking the north fork to Cwm Penmachno before descending through Cwm Hafodyredwydd, crossing over the Afon Machno at Rhyd-y-gro and approaching the village of Penmachno from the south-west. This valley is known a Y Wybrnant – a place once home to a dragon in myth. A stone found here in Penmachno is easily dated to 540 AD, even with half of the inscription missing. It refers to the 'son of Avitorius setting up the stone in the time of Justinius the consul'; another inscribed stone from the south-west extremity of the valley features the chi-ro symbol – the Greek letters for 'P' and 'Ch' resembling an 'X' with a superimposed 'P', meaning Pax Christi, or the Peace of Christ. This stone, known as the Carausius stone, is the only known memorial from the early mediaeval period used to mark a cairn-like grave – a pile of stones – as the inscription informs us. A holy well dedicated to Tudclud is situated in the village, in the cellar of the old post office (now a private residence).

Since there is only evidence of there being a chapel at Pentrefoelas in the sixteenth century, an

St Mary Magdalene's Church at Cerrigydrudion; a church has been on this site since at least 440 AD.

early link is not clear here, though the route is best served by taking the mountain track east from Penmachno to Dol Gynwal, later to become Ysybty Ifan, formng the route later used by drovers. The next stop at St Mary Magdalene's in Cerrigydrudion has had a church on the site since at least 440 AD, reputedly founded by Evanus, a disciple of St Patrick, and mentioned in 1254 in the Norwich Taxation. Maintenance and enlargement was carried out in 1503, and restoration work in 1874. (9)

The way onward to the church at Clocaenog (now under the patronage of St Foddhyd, with St Meddwyd and St Trillo having previously been associated) heads north-easterly by way of tracks about the course of the present B5105, before Derwen and Bettws Gwerfil Goch came to prominence on the north–south pilgrimage road. Clocaenog has had a church on the same site since the sixth century, though the present building dates from the thirteenth century, and further restoration was carried out in 1856. Victorian restoration features in many of the churches on most of these routes.

The destination of the route is cited as Chester, but why? The onward route could be lead to a number of possible variations, and Llanfair Dyffryn Clwyd on to Llanarmon yn Ial would also provide a suitable trajectory for the traveller aiming at Chester. What was the point of reaching

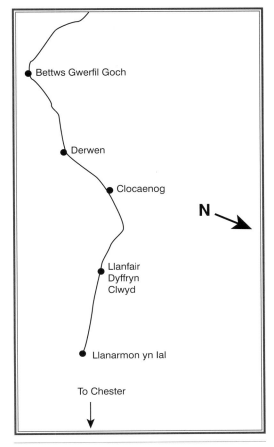

Map 2

Chester? In the Roman period as a legionary base with an attendant civilian settlement outside the wall, its attractiveness would be obvious. Recent excavations at Chester showed that its amphitheatre (in the final phase) was without equal in Britain, leading to the conjecture that it may have served as the northern capital of Roman Britain. Certainly it was a key part of the communication network in Britain for several centuries; for anyone with a message or a mission, Chester would have been an attractive point from which to gain access into the rest of Britain from the west. However, after the military departure in the early fifth century the focus of the population shifted from within the walls to an area around the amphitheatre and the River Dee until the tenth century. The church of St John the Baptist was not founded until the seventh century, most likely by the Mercian king Aethelred. It later became Chester's first cathedral between 1075 and 1541 after its promotion by Bishop Peter, the first Norman bishop of Mercia. (10)

There was also a church on the site of the second cathedral, into which were placed the relics of St Werburgh in 907. What was it that may have brought people to Chester along this route as early as the fifth century? One of the most stunning finds of the Chester Amphitheatre archaeological dig in 2006 was a large stone block almost in the exact centre of the arena, with a lead plug and a shorn-off iron ring. This would have been to tether combatants, animals – or maybe even potential martyrs – to keep them central to the spectacle of the amphitheatre for all to observe. Is it possible that the stone was used for executions and martyrdoms? The proximity of St John's church, and a strong consistent relationship between it and the amphitheatre, may indicate an earlier shrine or chapel in honour of those who lost their lives for their faith at the site– and such a chapel may form part of a reason for a pilgrim route.

Pilgrimage to Bardsey Island (Ynys Enlli)

The most famous and probably the largest-scale pilgrimages in North Wales involve Bardsey Island on the tip of the Lleyn Peninsula. Its earliest holy origins are debated, but its first significant visitor is thought to be Einion Frenin (the older brother of St Seriol) in the early fifth century. In 520 AD, St Cadfan established a monastery here. With the layers of saint upon saint claimed to have been buried here the isle went on to have a reputation so holy that it is thought many thousands of pilgrims came to visit on pilgrimage, for hundreds of years. It could be referred to as the 'Rome of Britain', or the "land of Indulgences, Absolution and Pardon, the road to heaven and the gate to paradise" (11). In the twelfth century Pope Callixtus II equated three pilgrimages to Bardsey with one to Rome, and later the same century, Giraldus Cambrensis remarked on the pilgrims on the trail to Ynys Enlli.

The tethering stone discovered at the centre of Chester Amphitheatre. Was this the focus of executions and Christian martyrdoms, giving the earliest relationship between the amphitheatre site and the later St John's church?

One must question the scale of the proposed pilgrimages to Bardsey. Upon reflection, what infrastructure could have been in place for providing hospitality for hundreds, if not thousands of people along the way? Depending on the exact route taken, how would the pilgrims have undertaken the hazardous crossing of the Conwy and Penmaenmawr headland en route to Bangor? How much money would be needed for travellers to make the pilgrimage and sustain them there and back (either travelling on foot, or by horse)? What large-scale provision of boats would have been available to taxi pilgrims across to the island? Resting on the assumption that the kitchen at Aberdaron was enlarged and able to cater for 1,300 people when operating at maximum capacity, how would one ferry 1,300 pilgrims in small boats across hazardous waters to an island with limited capacity? There are serious issues of supply-chains and logistics.

Once on the island, how would so many visitors be provided for in terms of accommodation, food, drink, and sanitation? Bardsey is literally an insular community and would need a steady supply of provisions to function as a 'retreat centre', as it would probably be called nowadays. Mainland-based places of pilgrimage require considerable effort and infrastructure to support their endeavours; if Bardsey really was the North Welsh equivalent of Santiago de Compostella, or only a rung or two down from Rome, thought needs to be given to such practicalities of logistics and the effects on the island of the proposed volume of pilgrims.

However, no demeaning of the pilgrimage to Bardsey is intended. None of the above is to say that pilgrimage did not happen, merely to question its scale and extent. For those who have stood on the tip of the Lleyn and considered these things, the island does indeed possess an alluring aura. When reading of ferrymen who would pause and bow their heads on close approach to the island, one can understand the deference offered to the locale. It is special. It is holy – for 'holy' means it is something 'set apart'. Bardsey is very physically removed from the mainland and therefore psychologically and spiritually set apart from the rest of Wales. Understanding the landscape and how it affects the perception of sense of place can enlighten us as to how locations like Bardsey, already with a considerable feeling of being special, can interact with the human mind and spirit with resulting experiences of the spirit of the place – the *genius loci* – whether taken literally or in the general sense. The same understanding can be applied to visits to any ancient sites, from prehistoric tombs to Roman temples, churches, and even landscapes with waterfalls and hills. The layering and perception of the sacred is still there to be experienced. Sacredness depends upon the nature of the place and its interaction of those in it – not upon the volume of visitors.

Another point to ponder concerns interaction with the special places on the Lleyn Peninsula which existed before Christians began making journeys past them. In a land like the Lleyn (and Anglesey) which is littered with megaliths, one wonders what the pilgrims' attitudes would have been to the ancient stones and cromlechs which they passed en route. In some places folklore which linked the stones to diabolical activity led to such places being held with superstitious regard, and on occasion left them open to harm or destruction. Given the superstitious mindset characteristic of perception in the Middle Ages, one would expect some anecdotes to have been handed down about some sites, and other sites to have perished as the result of prejudiced minds and fearful beliefs (although it is probable that such fears may have kept some of the stones in place). (12) Anglesey and the Lleyn possess both megaliths and early Christian sites in abundance. A sympathetic or at least a respectful attitude must have existed in those settling in and travelling through such prehistoric landscapes.

There are two pilgrim routes to Bardsey; one follows the north of the peninsula coming from Bangor, the other arrives from the south, either via an inland route (see the route to Chester, above) or along a coastal route past Tywyn from Pembrokeshire. Regarding their more northern origins, where might these routes be coming from? The northern route, if it began in Chester, as noted, would have had the famed horrors of the North Wales coast to deal with. Utilising an inland route, perhaps heading from Holywell to St Asaph and looping via Betws y Coed, the mountain passes of Snowdonia must be negotiated. If the pilgrims remained closer to the coast passing through such places as Llandudno (long before the railways opened it up to become the largely Victorian resort we see today), then the Conwy crossing and Penmaenmawr pass are unavoidable – except by a lengthy detour.

An easier approach would be similar to the route given from Chester, avoiding the worst of the mountains and the estuaries. Even with a departure north-west from Ffestiniog avoiding the tidal crossing at the Glaslyn (a path similar to some of the drovers' routes, but in reverse), there is still a need to avoid the expanse of the marshes south of Pont Aberglaslyn, and also a rough path west from Prenteg. If the pilgrims chose to stay south of the estuary, it would still need to be crossed with haste and agility at low tide. The picture of lame, crippled or self-chained penitents hobbling across the sands and fording the waters makes a questionable interpretation of this route into the Lleyn.

Whichever way the pilgrims passed through Snowdonia, there are then a host of possible sites which may have featured on their way. A number of guides already exist to take the modern pilgrim through the possible practices of the pilgrim of antiquity. In order to avoid replication of this information and focus upon the routes, what follows constitutes the basic information as to the possible routes, sites of note (to show the length of time a place has been 'holy'), and waymarkers or features which could have been notable for the pilgrims on their way. Not all the sites would have been visited by all the pilgrims.

The Pilgrim's Way to Bardsey (Northern Route)

Assuming a start in Chester at the easternmost extremity of the northern approach (and maybe for the southern approach, too), St John's church in Chester was noted in the thirteenth century for its important relic, the Rood of Chester. This was a silver gilt crucifix allegedly incorporating some wood from the 'True Cross', possibly brought back from the Crusades by Earl Ranulph III. A lot more could

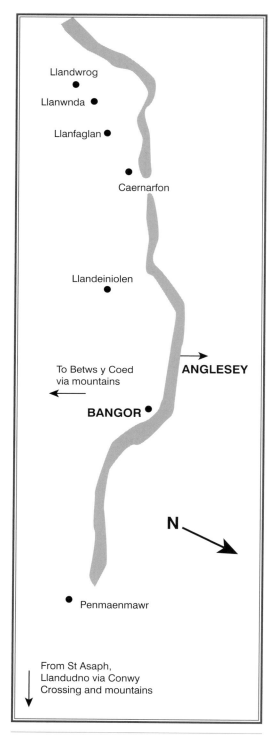

Llandwrog

Llanwnda

Llanfaglan

Caernarfon

Llandeiniolen

To Betws y Coed
via mountains

ANGLESEY

BANGOR

N

Penmaenmawr

From St Asaph,
Llandudno via Conwy
Crossing and mountains

Map 3

be said concerning the Rood of Chester, which was said to have been venerated by the Welsh, some even making a dedicated pilgrimage to see it. (13) Westward to Holywell and Winefride's Well would have been a required stop along the way (see below). The pilgrims would have headed to St Asaph with its cathedral, founded in the sixth century by Saint Kentigern who began a missionary training centre there in 560 AD. Thirteen years later he left to become the Bishop of Glasgow, leaving a pupil in charge: St Asaph. Pilgrims going through St Asaph used the bridge further downstream before the seventeenth century; the existing bridge is believed to have been constructed under the auspices of Joseph Turner in 1771 to replace the former bridge which was damaged in 1767. West again at Betws-yn-Rhos, a 'bede house' (commonly held to be the meaning of Betws) was situated next to the Roman road, where people could offer wayside prayers with their beads (i.e. rosaries). Taking the route via Betws-yn-Rhos would require a passage across the Conwy; see discussion above.

Closer to the main gathering point, St Tegai's church at Llandegai near Bangor was founded after a sixth century saint; the churchyard has a row of ancient yew trees, though the church itself is fourteenth century in the earliest part of its current structure.

Bangor Cathedral, which was the first cathedral in the country, would have been the most significant meeting place for this northern approach; it was founded in 525 AD by Saint Deiniol, who was later buried on Bardsey.

Progressing south from Bangor to Pentir and Llandeiniolen, then west to Llanbeblig, the pilgrim reaches the site of an early church a short distance downhill from the Segontium Roman fort at Caernarfon. St Peblig was a son of Elen Luyddog of Segontium, and thus very much a local character, though he travelled much further afield. The Christ of Caernarfon Rood was sited here, and must have been an obvious attraction. Maen Beuno, the cross-incised stone now at Clynnog Fawr, was situated here at Bryn Seiont in Caernarfon prior to removal.

The next stop is Llanfaglan; unusually this church was not subject to extensive renovations in the nineteenth century, so furnishings from the preceding century survive. The earliest part of its structure is thirteenth century, and aerial photography shows a complex layout of cropmarks about the church; perhaps this is the earliest 'llan' part of the church. St Baglan was a sixth century saint, and the church contains a contemporary inscribed stone. Baglan's Well is north-west from the church at SH460609.

The next two possible stops are quite recent structures very likely on the site of earlier buildings. At Llanwnda there is Saint Gwyndaf's church, dating from 1847, and Saint Twrog's church

The early mediaeval incised wheeled wayside cross at Capel Uchaf.

at Llandwrog (also linked to Maentwrog near Ffestiniog) is a Victorian structure built within a defining circular mediaeval enclosure.

At Capel Bettws ('Chapel of Prayer') was another mortuary chapel used to house the deceased on their way to be buried at Bardsey. Here again some doubt as to this practice should be pointed out; carrying a corpse for a considerable distance, unless death occurred en route, would be a difficult endeavour for the common pilgrim. If the death had occurred some time previously, thus allowing excarnation before the pilgrimage, the disarticulated skeleton would be easier to transport.

There is a roadside cross at Capel Uchaf (High Chapel) SH430499 – is this one of the 'meini cred', a creed stone where one might cross oneself and be reassured of divine protection? (14) Probably removed from its original situation, its current hazardous position now serves as a reminder that those passing this way in earlier times were using a means of transport more amenable to noticing minor wayside details.

A short distance further on to the south-west is the very important site of Saint Beuno's at Clynnog Fawr. Begun as a monastery in 616 AD by the eponymous saint; the church came into being around 630 as a hybrid monastery-cum-college, known technically as a 'clas'. There is much of note here; a free-standing slab-dial following the Anglo-Saxon system of breaking the day into eight segments is on the south side of the building. It is actually part of an Irish series of such dials and the only specimen of its type in Wales, originating between the tenth and twelfth centuries. The Maen Beuno cross-incised stone is now here, and an arch believed to have been part of the Tomb of St Beuno, demolished in 1856. Having bathed at St Beuno's Well, pilgrims would sleep on his tomb to (hopefully) effect healing. Given the size of tombs, how many pilgrims at one time could do this? If only one, then there are limited opportunities during the year for pilgrims to do this. St Beuno's Well lies a short way out of the village on the left-hand side of the road, requiring great care nowadays to visit; the volume and speed of the traffic risk ending any modern-day pilgrimage prematurely.

Progressing between the mountains, St Aelhaearn's church and well at Llanaelhaearn mark the branching of the route south-west for Bardsey. St Aelhaearn ('iron eyebrow') is a seventh century saint, after whom is named the village and church. An ancient site, the church was comprehensively

The road to Clynnog Fawr and St Beuno's church, now even busier than could ever have been experienced by pilgrims, and soon to be diverted past the village; Tre'r Ceiri visible top right.

St Beuno's Well on the road south of Clynnog Fawr; one of several wells associated with St Beuno across North Wales, and one of many others which could be visited by the pilgrim on the way to Bardsey.

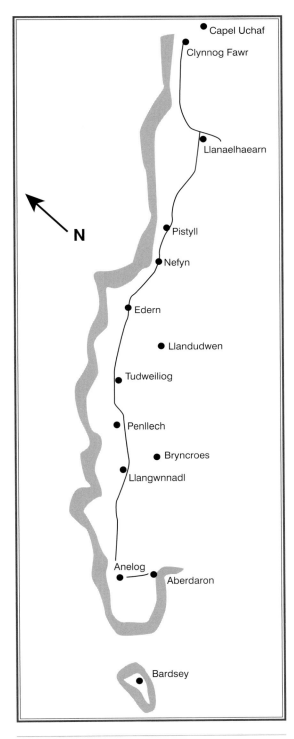

Map 4

remodelled in 1892, though a number of early gravestone inscriptions are to be found both outside and inside the church. The well is up-hill on the south side of the road, and can still be visited, as the pilgrims' way passes between the awe-inspiring mountains of Tre'r Ceiri and Mynydd Carnguwch. (15)

The next stop is just north of the main road (the B4417) at Pistyll; excepting the slate roof, the fabric of the church may be twelfth century. Another church originally dedicated to St Beuno, there was a monastery adjacent to the church, with an inn and waiting place at Eisteddfa field and Cae Hospice field (field of the hospice) (16). Lepers may have been accommodated at Cae Hospice Pennla. There is an eleventh century Anglo-Scandinavian interlace design upon the church's font, and there is a well referred to locally as simply 'the holy well' east of the church and uphill at SH330423. (17)

Exiting Pistyll, in the wall on the south side of the road is an eighth or ninth century cross-incised stone; it was moved between 1968 and 1971, with a previous known move before 1860, originally being a short distance to the south-south-west. (18) Three other cross-incised stones are referred to between Pistyll and Nefyn. (19)

At Nefyn, the church of St Mary was founded by Nefyn himself about halfway through the sixth century; it is now a museum. St Mary's Well in the centre of Nefyn was rebuilt in 1868. West again is St Edern's church (in Edern) which is thought to post-date a much older site within the village, though the current structure dates from 1867–8 with some parts as old as the fourteenth century.

South from Edern are two small early sites, St Ceidio's church (SH288382), with nearby place names of Plasyngheidio and Ceidio Bach indicating a wider association with the saint, and then further south again, Llandudwen (SH274369) north-east from Carn Fadrun. Here is St Tudwen's church, the current structure of which dates from 1595 although it was built on earlier foundations. There is a basin for a holy well, Ffynnon Dudwen, at

SH275368. (20)

At Tudweiliog the church's patrons are St Cwyfan from the seventh century and St Brigid; the building is probably another rebuild from the 1800s upon an earlier site. St Cwyfan's Well is mentioned nearby, reputed to have healed warts, eyes, and ague.

At Penllech (SH220344) there is another dedication to St Mary; the building has a Georgian interior but is in situ upon mediaeval foundations. South of Penllech and east of Llangwnnadl there is a holy well is dedicated to Lleuddad (SH220327), and yet another well further south – Ffynnon Fair (SH227314) has steps possibly dating from the seventeenth century, and is associated with St Mary's church in Bryncroes which has some roof trusses dated at least as early as the sixteenth century. (21)

South-west from Penllech is Llangwnnadl, named after Saint Gwynhoedl. It still has the site of the saint's shrine indicated by an inscription upon a pillar within the church, which in turn shows signs of having been enlarged. There is a field entitled "Cae Eisteddfa" – another waiting place for pilgrims to gather, perhaps. A large Celtic cross on a stone was found here in 1940, with traces of paint still surviving. It is dated to circa 600 AD; originally many of these ancient crosses were not the bare stone we view nowadays, but instead were colourful and attractive landmarks or religious 'art', often with a story to tell in their design and illustration.

St Merin's church, north of Capel Anelog (SH156274) was abandoned after the Reformation (SH173315). At Anelog, investigation in 1956 showed two robber trenches indicative of a small building, with all the foundation stones having been removed for reuse. (22) Two inscribed stones were taken to Cefnanmlwch before 1859; known as the Senacus Stone and the Veracius Stone, they were moved to the church at Aberdaron in 1990.

Not every place mentioned above would have been visited, though all have been in use for some considerable time. Different pilgrims would have varied their routes as individual circumstances, and those of the time and the respective places, dictated. After Bryncroes, a truncated route omitting Anelog can be postulated to rendezvous with the southern route to Aberdaron.

The Pilgrim's Way to Bardsey (Southern Route)

It was not until 1189 that the Knights of St John settled in Dol Gynwal as it was then known. They set up a hospice, which had entirely different connotations in usage then. Their hospices were there to offer hospitality – help, refreshment and accommodation to travellers such as pilgrims and drovers – as well as to host cattle fairs. Situated on a crossroads linking London, Anglesey, Bardsey and Chester, it was a prudent choice as a place for fairs to happen – though given its quiet rural demeanour on the banks of the Conwy one would not think so today. The parish church built on the site of the hospice has some significant alabaster effigies: Rhys Fawr ap Maredudd who bore the standard for Henry VII at the Battle of Bosworth; Rhys' wife Lowri, and their son who was crucifer and chaplain to Cardinal Wolsey.

Pilgrims passing through here either from Chester or approaching from the south-east, from Shrewsbury or Welshpool, would find themselves heading towards the Lleyn via Ffestiniog, possibly meeting those who had gathered on the coastal route further south at Tywyn. Here pilgrims would have to face the tidal crossing at Glaslyn, or a longer circuitous route – a diversion which is often overlooked by today's traveler in the comfort of motor transport and aided by embankments. In earlier times, getting to the Lleyn was for those happy to take long walks, or get wet and take risks with the tide.

Ffynnon Ddunawd (SH514401), north-west of Pentrefelin, is the first holy well to be reached, and would be the nearest holy spot actually on the Lleyn for those having made a tidal crossing in the Borth y Gest region. It is a much longer approach for those passing through the mountains, but

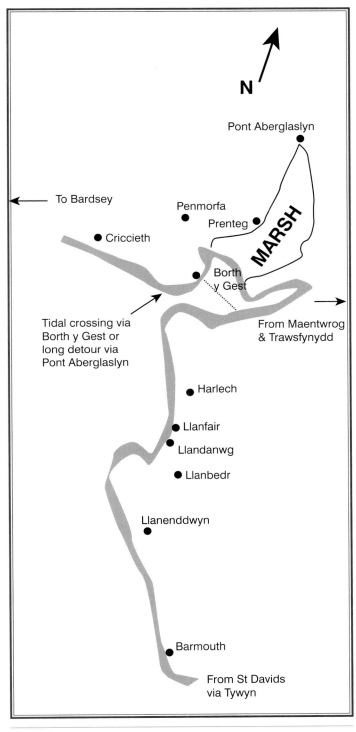

N

Pont Aberglaslyn

To Bardsey

Penmorfa

Prenteg

MARSH

Criccieth

Borth
y Gest

Tidal crossing via
Borth y Gest or
long detour via
Pont Aberglaslyn

From Maentwrog
& Trawsfynydd

Harlech

Llanfair

Llandanwg

Llanbedr

Llanenddwyn

Barmouth

From St Davids
via Tywyn

Map 5

if pilgrims on that route used the passes taken by the drovers they would still pass by here on the way to Criccieth, site of a Welsh castle with Edward I's English additions. A considerable distance north from here, at Llystyn Gwyn (SH482455), is an early mediaeval inscribed stone, with an Ogham inscription (an early Irish alphabet) and a corresponding Latin text. (23)

In Criccieth, just east of the B4411, there was a well dedicated to St Catherine (also known as Ffynnon Saint), reputed to be able to heal eyes. This survived until the 1960s when a garage was constructed upon the site and the well filled in. (24) To the north-west is perhaps the most famous of all the wells in the region: St Gybi's Well (SH427413). This well had a neighbouring cottage purpose-built for pilgrims, the ruins of which remain today; Cybi was a Cornish saint whose main association in North Wales is with Holyhead (in Welsh, Caer Gybi). There is an early mediaeval stone incised with a cross at St Cybi's church (SH429412), and a sixth century cross at SH421410.

South from Y Ffor on the way to Abererch is Ffynnon Cawrdaf (SH393376), associated with St Cawrdaf and Cadfarch's church at Abererch (east of Pwllheli). This dates back at least as far as the thirteenth century and was linked with Beddgelert Priory from the fourteenth century. It had extensions and additions in the fifteenth and sixteenth centuries, and possibly has a

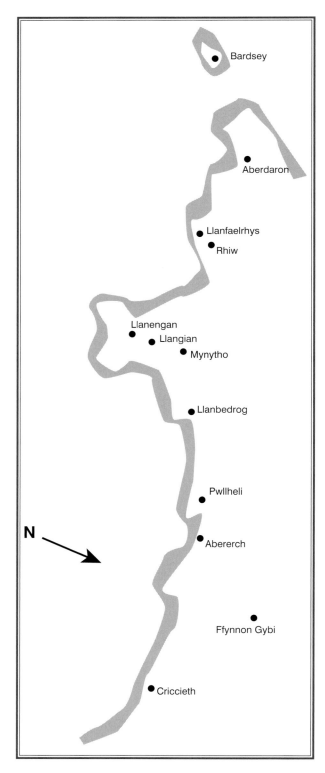

Map 6

chancel roof of the eleventh century.
(25) St Cawrdaf was a disciple of St Seiriol in the sixth century. Abererch is believed to be a place where those who had
become ill on the journey, or who were
tired and needed rest, could recuperate;
there is yet another "Cae Eisteddfa" for
those waiting for the right circumstances
(health or weather) to proceed.

West of Pwllheli on the route that
avoids the lower marshy land is Ffynnon
Bedrog on the descent to Llanbedrog
itself. The well (at SH323323) has a
small rectangular surround and is still
known by the title of "Wishing Well"
– a continuing veneration of the site. In
Llanbedrog the church structure dates
to the thirteenth century in its earliest part; St Pedrog was a sixth century
saint, also active in Ireland, Cornwall
and Brittany. A gallery in the town was
reportedly home to a seventh century
stone from Llangwnnadl, a place on the
northern route.

South-west from Llanbedrog and east
of Mynytho, Ffynnon Fyw (SH309309)
is a holy well linked to St Curig (sixth
century), which was restored around
1890; it is enclosed, with seats, a main
bathing pool and a smaller section for
drinking water, and is reputed to have
cured blindness. (26)

Onward to Llangian; the church here
is dedicated to St Cian, and may well be
of thirteenth century origin since it is referred to in a document dated 1254 (27),
though there are many additions and
alterations from the fifteenth and nineteenth centuries. There is an inscribed
stone in the churchyard at SH296289,
thought to be fifth or sixth century.

Llanengan is one of only two churches
on the southern route which look across
to Bardsey; most of the church fabric
dates from 1520–34, with additions and

changes during the past two hundred years. It is interesting to note the date of the fabric rebuilding and the date of the dissolution of the monasteries which affected Bardsey; it has been suggested that bell, the choir stalls and the money box may have come from Bardsey after the dissolution. (28) The well, Ffynnon Engan, survives with a basin and some masonry at SH293271.

To the north-west, low on the eastern slope of Mynydd Rhiw at SH242295, is Ffynnon Saint; a nine-foot-square pool survives here with an unnamed patron. Further south, Ffynnon Aelrhiw and his church are to be found. The present church is probably eighteenth century, but built upon an earlier site, with the well at SH23328. This is a seventeenth century basin with a stone platfom and seats surrounding. (29) A 'Delw Fyw' was also said to have occurred in the area – a living image of Mary which moved, much in line with both later and contemporary Marian apparitions. (30)

Llanfaelrhys' saint is St Maelrhys, with the church at SH210268 dating in its earliest phase to the mediaeval period (31); there is a well associated with the church at an unknown location.

At Aberdaron the routes converge as they cross to Bardsey; a second (surviving) Ffynnon Saint, three feet across with a lid of iron, is at the roadside north-west of Aberdaron (SH166267). (32) St Hywyn's and St Lleuddad's church at Aberdaron was the last stop before departing for Bardsey, with a waterside kitchen reportedly set up in 1300 to cater for pilgrims before they made the crossing to conclude the pilgrimage. The church originally had a round churchyard which was lost to the sea; it was also one of the sites designated as a 'clas' soon after its founding by Saint Hywyn, who was a contemporary of Cadfan.

Housed at Aberdaron is the Senacus Stone, found at Capel Anelog along with the Veracius Stone. The former has a late fifth century burial inscription upon an elongated triangular face, with the words SENACUS PRESBITER HIC IACIT MULTITUDINEM FRATRUM. This has been used to partially explain the legend of twenty thousand saints having been buried upon Bardsey. How one arrives at such a number from Senacus' 'multitude of brothers' is open to question. Another problem is that if this is a fifth century stone denoting multitudes, it predates St Cadfan's founding of the monastery; even dating the memorial to the later fifth or early sixth century does not give much time for such large numbers of holy persons to rest upon the land. (33)

A variety of means were provided to accommodate the pilgrims awaiting favourable conditions and transport to Bardsey, and in the event of a delay, two further possibilities for pilgrimage presented themselves to the traveller: St Mary's chapel, now almost completely destroyed, and the hazardous St Mary's Well (SH138253) which issues from a cleft in rock below high-tide level. In some conditions the water immediately surrounding it in the sea is freshwater, not saltwater. In legend it is suggested as one of three locations in Wales where Mary came ashore, leaving a footprint in the rock.

Bardsey's Welsh name, "Ynys Enlli", means 'the island in the current or tide'; waiting for suitable conditions would be imperative for those wanting to cross safely. Most would do so from Porth Meudwy to Cafn Enlli –(the Trough of Bardsey), a sheltered landing stage just east of the narrowest part of the island – a distance of about three miles, taking two hours to row across in fair weather–. How long pilgrims stayed on Bardsey and the details of their return journeys are not discussed, though if pilgrimage happened on the scale historically assumed, the island must have had some supply-chain solutions for even the most basic of requirements.

Holywell to St David's

A pilgrimage road less open to logistical problems by virtue of its situation, beginning in north-east Wales and with no sea or estuary crossings en route, was that between two giants of Welsh history, St Winefride and her well in Flintshire, and St David's in Pembrokeshire.

In the north, Holywell is situated not far inland from the Dee estuary, and is arguably the most spectacular of the holy wells in presentation and history. It has received uninterrupted pilgrimage

The sixteenth century façade of St Winefride's at Holywell; in terms of presentation and length of continued pilgrimage, there is no equal in North Wales.

since the seventh century, and has a well-housing without parallel. The forceful torrent of icy water domes up within a star-shaped chamber beneath a sixteenth century Gothic chapel. Steps into a bay resembling a baptistery descend in front of the chamber, and the water then flows into a large bathing area within which is Beuno's stone.

The legend of Winefride and Beuno and the story of the well's foundation (conferring sacredness in Christian eyes) is seventh century in origin, but such a spring would have been venerated by the Romans and ancient British too (like of the warmer waters of Sulis Minerva at Bath). (34) Winefride (in Welsh, Gwenfrewi), was the daughter of noble folk, and a devout woman. One day (Midsummer's day according to some sources – which could be of significance in the legend), while she was at her devotions a man named Caradoc appeared to seek refreshment. However, on spying the beautiful maiden before him he was overcome with lust and sought to force himself upon her. She fled to a nearby chapel where her uncle Beuno was praying. In the most dramatic of scenes, Caradoc, having followed her, drew his sword and decapitated her in the doorway, her head rolling a short way away. Beuno emerged and cursed Caradoc, reducing him to a puddle which drained into the earth; where Winifred's head was rent from her bod, a gushing of water emerged, and the place where Beuno then restored her head to her body is marked by the sub-aquatic Beuno stone.

It is not surprising that such a compelling story has maintained a large and long cult of veneration and worshippers. Winefride and Beuno also have other wells throughout Wales and the Welsh Marches. There are wells attributed to St Beuno at Holywell (largely overgrown) and at Bala (now dry), Gwyddelwern (encased and not very attractive), Tremeirchion (which emerges in an interesting head spout), Clynnog Fawr in conjunction with a standing stone (see above), and Maen Beuno south of Welshpool.

Winefride went on, it is said, to have a profitably godly life, establishing her community at Gwytherin nestling in the moors. There is a more modern church there now, but it situated on a mound with a stream running immediately adjacent, large yew trees surrounding it in the churchyard, and four reportedly prehistoric stones upon its northern side – though one bears an early mediaeval inscription. On her (second) death she was initially buried at Gywtherin, but her body was later moved to Shrewsbury Abbey, with a new holy well springing up at each place they stopped for the night (at Clutton south of Chester and at Woolston in Shropshire near Oswestry; a St Wenefrede's Lane north of Whitchurch further records this tradition). A pilgrim route marked by yew trees was said to have led from Gwytherin to Holywell, via Nantglyn, Henllan and Bodfari.

A pilgrimage road from Holywell to St David's bore across Wales on a south-west–north-east axis: "The road commencing from Holywell crossed the lower part of the Clwydian range of mountains, passing between Caerwys on the right and Ysgeifiog on the left, and descending by the present mountain-road by Bron Fox (so called from the sign of a way-side inn), it continued along the present narrow by-road, passing under Llangynhafal Church, until it reaches Ruthin, whence it continued

by a route under the Castle and over the side of Coed Marchan. A portion of it has been since stopped up. After bearing to the right, and leaving Derwen Church, it reaches Bettws Gwerfyl Goch; and if the common name of Bettws is a corruption of Bedehouse, this may have been a halting-place. About seventy years ago this now deserted and somewhat dangerous road for respectable carriages was the only available one. The road continued southwards at some distance from the present line, until it reached Bala: and keeping the lake on the right hand side, it followed the present line to Bwlch y Groes." (35)

To provide some expansion on the route departing from Ruthin: bearing south-west, the pilgrim road went through at Clocaenog which had a fifteenth century inn for hospitality for pilgrims (as well as an earlier church structure). The route then went on to Derwen, where just north of the church is St Sara's Well (also Saeran, an Irish Saint). In the churchyard is an impressive late fif-

The fifteenth century preaching cross in St Mary's churchyard, Derwen, en route from Holywell to St David's.

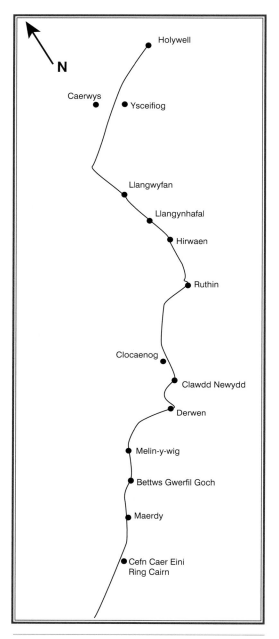

Map 7

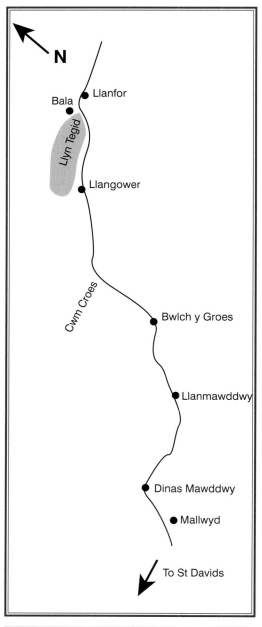

Map 8

teenth century preaching cross; the church retains many features of antiquity, worth investigating.

Pilgrims would then have gone on to Melin-y-wig, past a creed stone (wayside cross) near Pont Petryal on Cefn Bannog. (36) At Bettws Gwerfyl Goch there was a 'prayer house' originally credited to Gwerful the Red – a red-haired daughter of Cynan (37) from the late twelfth century. A holy well once existed at SJ033466, along with a church, both dedicated to St Mary.

The site of the Bronze Age ring cairn and kerb circle at Cefn Caer Eini – used as a trackway marker by the ancient British and pilgrims between Holywell and St David's.

Maintaining a direct south-west course through Y Maerdy, the pilgrims travelled the ridgeway next to Caer Eini hillfort and passed the Bronze Age cairn and kerb circles, which had already marked the route for over three millennia. Llanfor, north of Bala, was the next key point, with St Deiniol's church predating 1254. The building was replaced in 1875 upon the older layout; an early mediaeval inscribed stone is incorporated into the tower. A holy well at SH939368 was said to have flowed through the churchyard. (38)

The road continues along the east side of Llyn Tegid to Llangower, named after St Cywair (also Gwawr). The church here is first documented in 1291, though it was later restored courtesy of the Victorians. The churchyard sits upon an embanked enclosure that predates what is seen today. The enclosure is oval in shape, being about 400 by 300 feet across its axes; the boundaries are clearly visible in aerial photographs, and are right next to the Lake Bala railway. A sizeable mound within the churchyard has been construed as a possible preaching mound. (39) There is a spring sited nearby with the name Ffynnon Gower, though its designation as a holy well is not certain; the holy well attributed to Beuno is on the other side of the lake, and would have been missed by pilgrims using this route along the east side.

A partly cross-county route is then taken to Bwlch y Groes – the Pass of the Cross, and the highest point on the route. The pilgrims could not have traversed too far east, as the territory becomes too high for the journey; joining the road from the north opposite Cwm Croes (the Coombe of the Cross) would seem the logical way for the pilgrims to continue on, based on topography and place name. From the windswept pass the way descends swiftly southwards to the green valley around

The hollow way along the prehistoric and Roman route above Rowen; the stone in the left bank has an almost invisible incised early cross, showing that the route was once used by early Christians too.

Llanymawddwy, on to Dinas Mawddwy, and narrowly bypasses Mallwyd on the west to reach Ab-erangell. The pilgrims would then have continued on across country to St David's on the tip of Pembrokeshire. (40)

Wales is indeed a 'holy country', with towns, villages, shrines, wells, wayside crosses, and pilgrim roads and trackways criss-crossing the land. There are other pilgrimage destinations and places of spiritual journeying, both local and long-distance, which cannot be done justice in this volume. Llanddwyn Island on Anglesey and Pennant Melangell in the Berwyn Mountains are just two of the local pilgrimage places; other longer-distance trackways are the mediaeval pilgrimage route from Beddgelert Abbey to Holywell, passing through Dolwyddelan, and a "mediaeval highway" from Conwy to Ardudwy; these, among others are worthy of further investigation.

CHAPTER 5

Drove Roads & Trackways

D roving was no imperial route march along Roman highways or a dash for the Holyhead ferry. It was a slow, considered plod in all weathers, moving livestock across country to market and slaughterhouse in an age when the likes of cattle transporters or refrigerated articulated lorries did not exist. The pace was steady on foot, with the welfare and condition of the animals being of key importance. They needed to be alive and sellable at their destination. A variety of dramatic hazards faced those coming from north-west Wales in particular: mountain passes, tidal crossings, and even swimming the Menai Strait for those coming from Anglesey, were all required.

That the drovers traversed far and wide is evidenced by a certain Mr Bos, whom we shall meet again below, bragging that "…there are not many in Anglesey better known in England than myself – at any rate I may say that there is not a public house between here and Worcester at which I am not known." (1) From the Norman Conquest until the pinnacle of droving in the eighteenth and nineteenth centuries, droves were to be encountered all over the country.

A typical drove may have consisted of 100 to 400 livestock with four to eight drovers (although sometimes as many as twelve), plus their dogs to keep the livestock in check and round up stragglers and wanderers. The dogs could provide company and security for their owners, but could also serve as an advance guard in warning drovers' wives of their return by running on ahead on the return route. A dog named Cailo, from Llandrillo, was one such faithful beast who would make his way home with his owner's pony saddle, while said owner travelled home from the trek in the relative comfort of a coach – a not-uncommon practice during the later time of droving. Proceeding with the cattle was no exercise in speed. Two miles per hour was the average, giving an achievable coverage of 15 to 20 miles per day. Should the cattle be driven hard sweating would damage their hides, and skin quality was important to maintain.

Drovers could only be married men, householders, and over 30 years of age; this was to demonstrate that they were not vagrants or hawkers wandering aimlessly from town to village. Considerable trust was placed upon them – economic survival and prosperity was

Drovers' monument at Newbridge on Wye.

not only the concern of the farmers whose flocks, herds and livestock they drove, but also of the shoeing stations, Drovers' Inns, markets, abattoirs and dining tables for those encountering the animals en route and at journey's end. Dishonesty could bring hardship or ruin for many, and attracted this unflattering memorial, originally in Welsh:

Obituary of a Drover – Twm o'r Nant 1710

"Under this stone lies an old drover dead.
Messed up his life by cheating instead.
Up yours, arsehole! That's enough said!
Lets see you cheat your way from this bed!"

A display in the Drovers Arms at Rhewl in the Vale of Clwyd reads: "The Welsh economy, from the twelfth century onwards depended on cattle. Wealth was measured according to the amount of cattle owned… intermittent warfare between the English and the Welsh led to heavy penalties of cattle. For example, in 1277, Llywelyn had to pay a fine of 3000 head of cattle… this indicates an extremely wealthy area, paying a fine of tremendous proportion. During times of peace, the Welsh cattle trade was imperative to the needs of England, and English money returned to Wales through the drovers who walked the cattle to London…". (Note: the Drovers Arms at Rhewl has many photographs of drovers, ways, drovers' money and extensive displays on droving; besides a good deal of information it still offers friendly refreshment to travelers. The two verses of poetry are also quotes from their displays.)

In 1725 alone, a record shows London as having consumed 187,000 pigs, 90,000 bullocks, 70,000 lambs and mutton, 60,000 calves and 52,000 suckling pigs – some 459,000 animals, very few of which could be reared and sustained in or near the capital.

Being a drover also required some strength and a great deal of fitness. The men had to cover considerable distances each day in every sort of weather and be fast enough to gain control of errant animals (and accurate enough to lasso where necessary – a vital skill for saving an animal's life if it was swept away by the waters when swimming the Menai Strait, for example). They also had to be strong enough to rope and wrestle with cattle for shoeing or branding. Even some veterinary knowledge would have been called for, to administer stitches and basic medical care to the animals. Anyone who has attempted to clean their dog's ears and knows how much of a struggle that can be can imagine what it must be like with to deal with an animal much larger and stronger than a dog.

On occasion, even digging a wilderness grave may have been necessary; if one of those working on the drove was killed by the physicality of dealing with an animal, or was trampled, practicality dictated that a corpse could not accompany the drove. A roadside burial was imperative, with, it is said, a tree planted to mark the spot.

It was important that drove stock did not become mixed with farm animals as they passed other fields and businesses not part of the drove. To assist in this, there would be a walker half a mile or so in front to shout a warning. This would (hopefully) enable farmers to get their own livestock out of the way, or prepare them to join the drove where necessary. It also gave warning to people, children in particular, to get out of the way, as several hundred animals were soon to be passing their way. Accidents were not unknown, and as road traffic increased this early warning became even more necessary: "In the stage-coach period, when the road to London was a thing of life, the Welsh drover, raising its dust with his herds of black cattle and ponies, was a prominent feature of the traffic." (2) The warning shout is recorded with variations depending on the sources. The Welsh yell would be "Heiptrw Ho!", with Anglicised corruptions being "Ho ho!" and even "Trobadoo! Trobadoo!". The calls have more of a phonetic primeval urge than any grammatical ushering out of the way.

Those with memorable yells could even end up with poetic lines remembering their capacious lungs and loud voices:

"Jonny Morris and his drovers
Could be heard above all others.
And Sylvanus Evans wisely
Always truthful, paid the money".

The drovers could have a number of followers and folk assisting with the transport of the animals. Besides the caller-out for warning villages and farms of their approach, there could be herders, possibly on horseback, to help deal with strays. Two people would follow the herd directly supervising the flow of animals, with the drover following on behind, again often on horseback, ensuring everything went as well as possible for the sake of his livelihood and that of all those associated with the drove. Packhorses or carriages may also have accompanied the droves; even the sons of rich landowners could journey alongside as a means of gaining experience along the way to visiting the big cities and towns.

Likewise, children and young ladies bound for domestic duties would be entrusted to the care of drovers who knew the journey and the destinations well. Jane Evans from Pumpsaint travelled with drovers to go and work with Florence Nightingale. Before a dedicated mail service arrived drovers could also function as postal carriers, taking news out and bringing word from the wider world back to obscure villages and towns on the way home. Drovers were the 'RSS feeds' of their time, to frame them in terms of today's up-to-the-minute news updates.

At the shoeing stations cattle had to be fitted with iron shoes (ie. shod), due to the effect of hard road surfaces on their cloven hooves; even geese which could accompany the droves received boots, which must have been something to see in action. Depending on the size of the drove, a stop at a major station could take several nights whilst the herd was shod; it may also have been necessary to wait for other cattle to catch the drove that had not yet joined the group. A man and boy could shoe between 60 and 70 cattle daily, so with a little mathematics, depending on the workforce a shoeing stop could turn into a reasonable stop-over. The work of shoeing, more accurately referred to as cueing after the name of the cattle shoes (cue, or in Welsh, cws), was a dramatic, energetic labour to perform. A looped rope would be cast over the beast then brought together near its feet, sweeping its legs from under it. The shoes were then nailed and angled into the hoof.

The twin shoeing of each of a Welsh Black's hooves was essential for the well being of the cow en route to market.

For security, the drovers' herdsmen would work in shifts to supervise the animals overnight; the opportunity for cattle rustling is obvious. Additionally, carrying substantial sums of cash on the return route having sold the livestock, the drovers could be easy prey for criminals. Some of the first bank arrangements were put in place to safeguard the economic interests of all concerned, with notes and cheques which could be exchanged for their real value at a later point. One of the local banks set up for this was the appropriately-named Banc y Ddafad Ddu – the Bank of the Black Sheep.

This did not safeguard all drovers, and with a long history of droving before banking was introduced there are many tales of murder or betrayal of the drovers and sometimes of those who travelled with them. On other occasions there were accounts of the drovers dramatically outwitting would-be thieves spotted in advance before they could accomplish their devious intent. Not all thieving would be due to mere dishonesty or the influence of Mammon – desperate times could generate desperate actions for those needing food, or money for food. The drover and his animals could be seen as an easy target. Great care was needed, but even that may not always have been enough.

A particularly epic story recounts that a drover and his helpers encountered a local cutthroat and his cohorts around Llandegla. When the drovers refused to yield to threats, they settled upon choosing a man from each of their sides to engage in mortal combat – with sickles. In the best tradition of heroic tragedy, the drover won the contest, but received wounds leading to his death after the fight. The hero and the villain were buried in a field which came to be known as Cefn y Beddau – the Ridge of the Graves. It is reported that their burial mounds were still visible into the 1900s.

Others were also unlucky, but not always so heroically. Around Dolgellau there was a bandit named Twm Ddu'r Twca (translating with the most threatening and terrifying of titles: "Black Billhook Tom"); he killed his victims, and burned their remains upon pyres of gorse and heather as his murderous trademark.

With the advent of toll roads many droveways took to higher or more difficult ground to avoid adding extra charges to their expenses. The list of tolls at the Bala to Dolgellau gate gives an idea of the additional pecuniary expenditure, which repeated again and again on different stretches of toll road would soon contribute, literally, to a heavy toll.

TOLLS taken at this GATE

For every Horse or other Beast drawing any Coach Chariot Chair with four or two Wheels 6D.

For every Horse or other Beast drawing any Waggon with four or two Wheels 4D.

For every Horse or other Beast laden or unladen and not drawing 1½ D.

For every drove of Oxen Cows or neat Cattle per score and so in proportion for any less number 10D.

For every drove of Calves Hogs Sheep Lambs or Goats per score and so in proportion for any less number. 5D.

An insight into the drover's world comes from George Borrow's famous encounter with Mr Bos on Anglesey, where Mr Bos is insistent that Borrow must be a 'pig-jobber' on account of his earlier visiting Llanfairpwllgwyngyll. Borrow describes Bos' outfit thus: "He was dressed in a pepper-and-salt coat of the Newmarket cut, breeches of corduroy and brown top boots, and had on his head a broad, black, course, low-crowned hat. In his left hand he held a heavy whale-bone whip with a brass head." (3) Their exchange yields useful information: " '…who but a pig-jobber could have business at Llanfair?', 'Does Llanfair produce nothing but pigs?' said I. 'Nothing at all… that is nothing worth mentioning. You wouldn't go there for runts…". (4). Runts are the Welsh Blacks which were the main cattle to come out of Wales. Runt in common use is a derogatory term at worst, and at best the designation of poor quality. Not so in this case. Welsh runts were small black cattle, but they were of good quality, able to deal with the lack of quality grazing along the way and remaining agile, but then quickly fattening up ready for slaughter after a short time of preparation for the table.

Speaking of the table, as seen above, the famed 'good old English roast beef' was often a product of Wales. Akin to the English castles in North Wales for which Wales is now famous, the reverse was true for quality meat from these Welsh Blacks.

Other animals did accompany the droves, sometimes in carts. Borrow met a gentleman near Llangollen with a large pig: "…I soon overtook a man driving five or six very large hogs. One of these which was muzzled was of a truly immense size, and walked with immense difficulty on account of its fatness. I walked for some time by the side of the noble porker, admiring it…'Those hogs are too fat to drive along the road,' said I… 'We brought them in a cart as far as the Pentre Dwr… but as they did not like the jolting we took them out.'" (5) Pigs were not driven far, averaging about six miles daily (perhaps that explains the aforementioned hog being carted), though sometimes they are reported to have had woollen boots with leather soles. (6)

Other animals featured in the droves, such as sheep – though not from far north-western Wales, with its greater amount of higher mountainous terrain to deal with, as well as swimming the Menai Strait or fording tidal rivers and estuaries at low ebb. Geese and turkeys also joined the throng on occasion from the eighteenth century onwards.

The pace of the drovers in the eighteenth century was affected by the growth of non-comformist Christianity, spreading with great passion and evangelistic, revivalistic fervour. As moving animals was work, doing so on a Sunday was certain to evoke not only the anger of those caught up in or leading the holy zeal of the times, but, it was claimed, also the wrath of God himself. To deter Sabbath breaking, penalties were said to have been brought in to safeguard the sinful drovers and their teams' souls in the next life. As with any legalistic endeavour, ways were found to work around the penalties, or at least minimise the effect they could have on the progress of the drove.

Tracing the drove routes can prove a particular challenge. The more southerly routes of North Wales and those in Mid Wales have been well covered in previous works. (7) Those in the the far north and east of the principality have hitherto been poorly described, and in comparison with the line of modern arterial roads the drovers' routes are not obvious due to their relatively indirect paths.

There is also an issue concerning at which point a path used for the movement of livestock becomes a drove route per se. It would be absurd to think of every livestock movement as defining such a route; just because animals may be driven along a given way does not make it a drove route. It is not just a matter of semantic argument, but of the definition of a highway which is appropriately designated a 'Drove Route'.

A useful metaphor is to think of the points at which raindrops come together, converging with other raindrops on a surface and through innumerable confluences becoming streams and rivers. Similarly one may think of drove routes coming together from multitudes of smaller meetings from individual farms and fields. These groups become increasingly larger until the force of thousands of hooves across the earth defines the course of their procession, as water defines the course of a river. Unlike a river, however, the further from their source the droveways journey and the more variables in their destination, the greater the opportunity for confusion and uncertainty.

The routes given below are the principal flows and starting points used by those men and animals undertaking the trek through Wales and England; indeed, of all the types of routes covered in this book is the drove routes are arguably the most epic and dramatic.

Bardsey to Penmorfa and Borth y Gest

Bardsey is notable as the extreme tip of the western supply route for droving on the Lleyn Peninsula. One must question the scale of the droves coming over from Bardsey. How many animals could be ferried across the perilous waters at one time? How many would be required for sustenance for the long-term residents? Or indeed, if the claims of large-scale pilgrimage to this most holy of Welsh places are true (see Chapter Four), would pilgrims have needed to bring over their own supplies of animals? If there really were thousands of visitors arriving monthly or annually, the island's own resources would have been stretched.

In the 1800s some 6,000 cattle left the Lleyn; east- and south-eastward-bound to supply English fairs. (8) The very first of the first droves from this western fringe would assemble at Aberdaron, then head north-eastwards along the quiet lane passing between Mynydd Rhiw and Mynydd y Graig. The

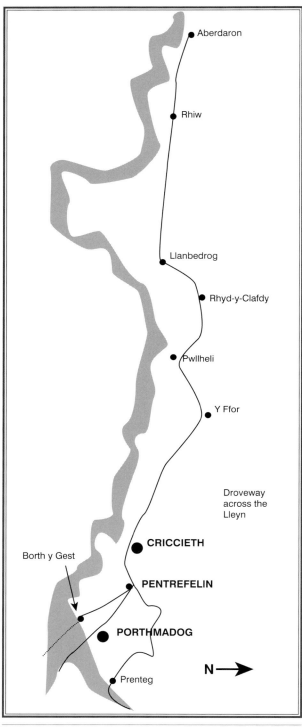

Aberdaron

Rhiw

Llanbedrog

Rhyd-y-Clafdy

Pwllheli

Y Ffor

Droveway
across the
Lleyn

Borth y Gest

CRICCIETH

PENTREFELIN

PORTHMADOG

Prenteg

N→

Map 1

former is host to a wide array of Bronze Age and Neolithic monuments including the Neolithic axe factory upon its north-eastern flank. Burial chambers, cairns and standing stones, hut circles and a fort are all clustered in the area.

Past Talafon with the expanse of Hell's Mouth beneath, the route curves to the north-east and then east again along the course of what is now the B4413, approaching but not entering Llanbedrog. The droveway then heads north curving into Rhyd-y-Clafdy, continuing by way of the B4415 to Efailnewydd. Taking the easterly arm at the junction, the route curves towards Pwllheli, remaining to the north of the town. Approaching Y Ffor from the south along the line of the A499, on the east side of the road is another Neolithic chamber. The drove route makes a decisive turn to the east (now on the B4354), through Chwilog, before merging with the A497 –at the site of an old toll gate. The droveway would have taken the course of the older north curve of the road, crossing the Afon Dwyfor at Llanystumdwy and continuing on through Criccieth. It curves north-east once more (a burial chamber lies just to the south of this curve) to Pentrefelin. On the south side of the road just opposite a fork in the route is a tall standing stone embedded in the tarmac of the pavement immediately adjacent to the roadside. Easily missed, the stone is of uncertain antiquity. (9)

Across the road from the stone, the north-east fork is the one some of the drovers would have taken. The way for those taking the tidal sand crossing from Borth y Gest before the Cob at Porthmadog was constructed, or indeed the through routes prior to Tremadog's existence, is unclear. However, examination of the map and deep-walled hollow ways both suggest a course bypassing the pronounced hill of Moel-y-Gest on the west and south, between numerous sites of Iron Age hut circles and a Neolithic burial chamber, approaching the sand and mud of Borth y Gest from the north-west or the north.

Penmorfa to Maentwrog

Just south-east of Penmorfa lies Porthmadog. Travelling from Porthmadog direct to Maentwrog was not possible until William Alexander Maddocks constructed the embankment known as Y Cob (the Cob) in 1811, facilitating an easier crossing towards Maentwrog. By the time he drained the Traeth Mawr in the 1820s there was already an eastbound turnpike in operation.

However, until then there were two possibilities for getting to Maentwrog with the droves. Firstly, to avoid the mountains without ending up on impassable marshes, the droveway swings around in a large loop with two crossings of the Afon Henwy and descends to Prenteg from the north and west, past innumerable Bronze Age burnt mounds and Iron Age settlements beneath Mynydd Gorllwyn. Heading north from Prenteg along the course of the A498 the drove would then cross the Aberglaslyn bridge. About one third of the way along this stretch, note the Turnpike Cottage on the east above the Afon Glaslyn. Returning down route of the A4085 from Nantmor, above Plas Brondanw a wide swing around the valley edge would be required rather than the straight crossing the current route affords. At Garreg the route takes a left (eastward) turn along the B4410 through Rhys (to cross the Afon Rhyd), through Bwlch y Maen between Fron Goch and Moel Llys, bringing the droves to Tan y Bwlch and Maentwrog.

Alternatively, it does not seem too much of an outrageous supposition for some droves, on occasion and with particular reason, to have joined the southbound droveway for Harlech across the sands from Borth y Gest, but then to have departed along the route of the A496 to the north of Cilfor. See below for more on the possible crossing points for this route.

Maentwrog to Bala (direct)

Having entered the Vale of Ffestiniog, a forking of the ways was possible, with the options of a direct route to Bala, a detour via Trawsfynydd, or a path by way of Ysbyty Ifan to Pentrefoelas and Cerrigydrudion. The first of these possibilities is now examined.

Those taking this route could stay north of the Afon Dwyryd on the old main road to Blaeneu Ffestiniog and Llan Ffestiniog until they reached Pont Dol-y-moch. After this point they would have followed the course of the B4391 to Llan Ffestiniog, with the south-curving continuation of the droveway heading east beneath Craig y Garreg Lwydm and then south-east beneath Moel Llechwedd-gwyn. The route passes the expanse of the Migneint to the north and then Carnedd Iago, joining the Trawsfynydd route between the Arenigs on the central ridge of the Cambrian

The standing stone of probable eighteenth century date, with the droveway departing to Penmorfa, rear left.

A deep hollow way runs between two drystone walls pointing to Borth y Gest and the Glaslyn Estuary for a well-timed crossing at low tide.

Mountains at Pont Rhyd-y-fen where it crosses the Afon Tryweryn.

These merged drove routes now pass one of two huge modern reservoirs which were not in the landscape until this past century. Llyn Celyn was built between 1960 and 1965, and flooded the valley, drowning the village of Capel Celyn to national Welsh outrage and boosting support for Welsh nationalism and the Plaid Cymru party. The insensitive driving-through of the bill to dam and flood the valley, ignorance of the objections of all but one of the Welsh MPs, and perceived suppression of Welsh language, culture and wishes in order to supply Liverpool with further water, all inspired acts of sabotage during construction and even during the opening ceremony. The microphone wire was cut during inaugural speeches: the voice of the Welsh may not be heard, so then neither shall the English. If one sees the graffiti "Cofiwch Dryweryn", it is an instruction to 'Remember Tryweryn'.

Given that drovers sought to avoid going through villages unless they were picking up further cattle, visiting a shoeing station, or getting an overnight rest, it is likely that they bypassed this now-lost village on the way to Bala, passing Mynydd Nodol to the south, through

Pont Dol-y-Moch on the old road from Maentwrog to Blaenau Ffestiniog – now a minor single track road

Llidiardau and past Ty'n-y-sarn –(the House on the Old Track) and briefly converging with the course of the A4212 before crossing an old crossroads just north of Bala itself.

Maentwrog to Bala (via Trawsfynydd)

This way would now loop along the routes of the A470 and the A4212, but which exact route the drovers took is uncertain, especially since some of it is likely no longer on dry land. A landmark of huge significance in North Wales' history over the past hundred years is the vast lake at Trawsfynydd, named after the village on its eastern side. Initiated in 1924 it is now the third largest lake in Wales, with a surface area of some 1,200 acres. Its purpose was to serve the Maentwrog Hydro Power Station which opened in 1928, a purpose which it still serves today, albeit with the power generation happening nearer to Maentwrog above the A496. The lake later provided cooling water for the nuclear power station which operated between 1965 and 1991 upon its northern shore. There used to be an informative visitors' centre which had to close for security reasons, and the site is under ongoing decommissioning work, scheduled to be complete in 2096.

Returning to the drove route, initially it would make most sense for the path to head through Gellilydan, avoiding the steep ascent of the modern A487 through Ceunant Llechrhwd. Linking the curves of the A487 by the east side, another faint track passes Llain Wen Farm and then leads to the principal road in Trawsfynydd. For the drovers heading east, the track and footpaths hugging the curvature of the field boundaries are likely to constitute an older route than the way to the north adjacent to the disused railway line. Crossing the Afon Prysor just below Glanllafar the drove route would then have run concurrent with the A4212 into Cwm Prysor, then east along the northern flanks of Craig y Hyrddod, between Arenig Fawr and Arenig Fach and through Rhyd-uchaf, finally meeting the more direct Maentwrog to Bala route.

Maentwrog to Corwen via Ysbyty Ifan

At the start this route shares the same passage as the line straight to Bala, but at Pont yr Afon Gam it heads north-east along the route of what is now the B4407. This is the bleak expanse of the Mi-

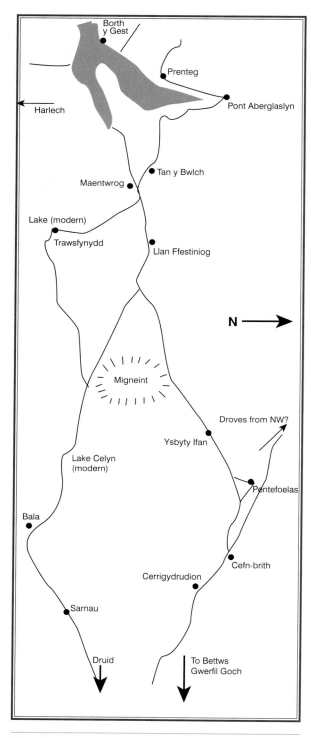

Map 2

gneint, and a clear road is imperative. The peat-cutting strips are a stark reminder of the swathes of peat and blanket bog that direct much of the passage of the traveller. Just over the Gwynedd / Conwy boundary on the west side of the road is a well, reconstructed in 1846. This is Ffynnon Eidda, a watering hole for droves on their way; as to its suitability for drinking after animals had used it, one must wonder. The reconstruction favours human access with a staggered approach. Nonetheless the Welsh inscription "Yf a bydd Ddiolchgar", meaning "Drink, and be thankful", would have been appreciatively greeted by thirsty drovers and their teams en route to Ysbty Ifan.

A little further on just on the inside of the fork to Penmachno is a milestone; both sides give mileage to respective destinations, and the exposed side is visibly more weathered than the sheltered side.

The number of small bridges to be crossed is indicative of the amount of water flowing off these mountains; on the first kink in the road after the well there is a former fording point – Rhyd Cerrig Gwynion. Three streams further on is the first crossing of the River Conwy at the Pont ar Gonwy, Llyn Conwy forming its source just to the north. Passing between the summits of Llechwedd Brynia Defaid to the north and Bryn Glas to the south, the inspiring massifs of the Arenigs are visible in the distant south-east.

The change from bog and moorland to lush grazing pasture soon becomes apparent when dropping into the Vale of Conwy on the approach to Ysbyty Ifan, where a firm bridge provides the second and last crossing of the Conwy on this route. Just before the bridge there is Penrhyn's Well, with milestones embedded further along in the same wall, on the wall opposite, and finally on the bridge. A corresponding empty niche on the south-east wall of the bridge seems to have held a now-eroded

Ffynnon Eidda well for drovers and droves for animals crossing The Migneint.

Milestone at the junction for Penmachno the The Migneint.

inscription.

Formerly called Dol Gynwal, Ysbyty Ifan was a home of St John's Hospitallers from 1190 onwards, and offered hospitality to pilgrims and drovers over the centuries. Taking the initial road on to Pentrefoelas, an apparent older route may be construed. The current route takes a wider arc to Rhydlydan north of Bryn Prys; where the modern surface veers more north-north-east, the earlier route continues on a north-east course. Just to the south of this pass is the mysteriously named Carreg y Blaidd – the Stone of the Wolf. One wonders what story, if any, lies behind this place name. The trackway then progresses through a narrow pass on the south of Bryn Prys.

Bromlow Callow in Shropshire; a droveway route marker visible for many miles around.

At this point, what may have been a drovers waymarker is visible to the north. To the north-east of Pentrefoelas look for a distinctive tree-circled hilltop. This is strikingly similar to Bromlow Callow in Shropshire, a well-known tree-topped hill which served drovers traversing the open country. Working on the assumption this is a drovers' marker, further credence may be given to another drove route coming from the north and joining the thrust towards Corwen. Dutton suggests that the track adjacent to the now-confused jumble of largely toppled Bronze Age stone rows at Hafod y Garreg was a drove route. (10) The possible hilltop marker would also be of service to drovers along this route, which can be projected to join the main route described here just before Cefn-Brith.

The route from Ysbyty Ifan has to cross three fording points before joining the course of the main road prior to the construction of the A5; these crossings occur at Rhyd-y-gau, Rhydlydan and Cefn Rhyd. At Glasfryn, the track would head to Cefn-Brith and onward to Cerrigydrudion, over Rhyd-y-groes. The road taken by the Telford's A5 did not exist at this earlier time; a clue to its later origin is the lack of housing clustering along the line of the road leading north-west from Cerrigydrudion. This was a vital stop along the way, as it served as a shoeing station for cattle that needed attention.

Whilst in this region and by way of indicating other droveways arriving around Pentrefoelas, a drove trackway is recorded on the first edition Ordnance Survey maps near Llyn Aled Uchaf south-east from Gwytherin at SH890608 (11); this is off the line of the main drove-routes, so may have been a localised route; nothing is visible of it as of 2003. However, given the context of the other two drove ways noted below, perhaps this could be construed as a drove route which would converge with the course of the A543, to join the route to Corwen or Ruthin at Rhydlydan.

Nearby is recorded a "pentagonal enclosure on the current and 1st edition OS mapping. The site was found to delineate a raised area of land and had the remains of a drove road running along its northern boundary." (12) This is at SH914582, between Aled Isaf and Llyn Aled. A further entry in the Coflein database (the third of three drove roads in this part of North Wales) records "The partially surviving remains of an old drove road running up over the moors in a roughly north/south direction. It measures 1.75m wide by 0.4m–0.5m deep. South end is SH8949160533, north end is

A tree-ringed hilltop above Pentrefoelas, strikingly similar to Bromlow Callow; is this a droveway marker for those coming from the north and from the south from Ysbyty Ifan?

SH8951860626." (13)

The way on from Cerrigydrudion to Corwen would best follow a short stretch of the B5105 (with the name Green Bank, suggestive of it having received ample fertiliser from animals). This route takes the same exit from Cerrigydrudion as that suggested by Toulson for the droves bound for Ruthin and Wrexham. The way then runs south-east beneath Caer Caradog (as previously noted, this is one of many so-named Iron Age hillforts), passing between Y Drum to the north and circling the northern slopes of Mwdwl-Eithin –(surmounted at its summit by a Bronze Age cairn) to begin its descent over the southern end of Moel Chwa. The droveway descends steadily to the Afon Alwen through Rhos-cae-r-ceiliog and Ty-Cerrig. Where Toulson suggests a southern loop, a lane, now fragmented, would cut off this detour, bringing the cattle down to Gro and the bridge into Bettws Gwerfil Goch.

Leaving Bettws by the south-east-facing road, and ascending very steeply on an easterly course, the surfaced road is now very deeply sited between two high banks, both walled with green verges and providing a wide passing space. A course for Gwyddelwern takes the route on the most agreeable way along some of the ridge below Cefn-ddwynant, emerging south of the next village. Bound for Corwen, an older route is traceable which swings around to join the A494 west of Ty'n-y-rhos, heading to the crossing of the River Dee past Ffynnon Sulien, arriving on the west bank at Pont Corwen.

The droves bound for Ruthin would turn northwards at the southern entrance to Gywddelwern, then leave the village by the road to the east opposite the church. Travelling progressively uphill and south-east, the droveway then follows the right-angled field boundary-cum-track north-east on a clear course north, taking the lower ground with three distinct summits to the right and three summits to the left. Intersecting the modern lane at Blaen Cwm, it continues north to Llanelidan

Looking down the broad lane north east from Bettws Gwerfil Goch, with high green banks enclosed with drystone walls, on a now well-surfaced broad hollow way.

The eastward approach to the major droving centre of Corwen as most now see it. Possible Neolithic cursus monuments, Bronze Age tracks, Roman roads and droveways all converge near here.

via Pentre, joining the course of the A494 south-west of Nantclwyd Hall. Some of the old ways are still visible here before the roads crosses over the River Clwyd. The final approach to Ruthin is along the Corwen road.

Corwen via Llangollen to Wrexham and Chirk

Bonser notes: "...every drover tended to vary his cross-country routes should he find an old one becoming too congested or the accommodation at the farms or inns no longer adequate... Most of the traffic from North Wales including that of the Lleyn Peninsula, went through Wrexham, long known as the Northern Gateway of Wales. Llangollen Fair, a few miles to the south-west, was an important centre for the cattle trade. Drovers came there from Bala, Corwen and Ruthin and other surrounding districts..." (14)

The question of the route from Corwen to Llangollen is a source of exasperation. Toulson's important work, whilst detailing accurate and interesting walks south of Llangollen, takes the drove routes across the Berwyn from Corwen (see below), but then abandons the route to Llangollen itself to the distant south, giving the impression that the track from Corwen to Llangollen was a hugely circuitous detour, or else leaving the question unanswered if Toulsen assumed the answer was obvious. Examination of the map would support the assumption that

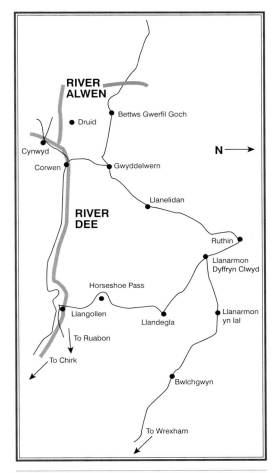

Map 3

livestock bound for Llangollen would travel on a route very much in keeping with the modern route based upon Telford's road and the coach road. The way onward would then cut to the north side of the bridge in Llangollen, making its way north-west past Ruabon to Wrexham.

It is in the Wrexham area that we find the most extensive entry for a drove road in the monuments database for North Wales. It does not fit in with the line of drove roads recorded as the major through-routes for livestock. At SJ272485 there is a note of a "...Stretch of drove road located to the south-west of Plas-yn-fron Farm. Shown on current OS mapping as a track. Has substantial earthfast stone and turf bank downslope on east side. The bank is about 2m wide by 2m high. It is constructed of small-medium sub-angular stone packed into an earth bank, with very old trees growing through it. The drove road is about 4m wide..." (15). The road follows a north–south axis, and is not apparently on a direct line towards Wrexham, Chester or Llangollen, insofar as this segment demonstrates. It seems to fit in better with a line from Coedpoeth to Penycae near Ruabon – perhaps linking with the western droveway descent to Wrexham from Bwlchgwyn. However, this would necessitate crossing the lower reaches and flows from Ruabon as well as the Esclusham and Minera mountains. Close reading of the map could render this a possibility.

The existence of a route from Llangollen to Y Waun (Chirk) bound for Oswestry and Shrewsbury is a certainty. Remembering George Borrow and the noble porker of great girth at Llangollen, these animals were bound for onward sale at Wolverhampton. It is on this route that a southbound way on to the ridgeway could make sense, if the drovers were not taking the steady ascent to Froncysyllte. Up Allt y Gwernant, a route exhausting in its steepness, then east past the stone of Carreg y Big, and finally dropping to England north-east of Chirk Castle would seem to be a reasonable passage for the droves. Onward travel is then straightforward, to Oswestry and Shrewsbury, the Midlands and London.

Bala to Corwen

The journey from Bala to Corwen is a route with several choices. It could take the route of the Roman road and the A494 well west of the Dee Valley to Llangollen, passing through Llanfor; near here was situated the Roman fort and the now-perished Bronze Age stone circle of Pabell Llywarch Hen (SH940366). The property next to this location is called Carreg y Big – the big stone (given its descriptive nature, this name occurs with some frequency). Passing between Bryn Banon and Cynlas, place name evidence is once more suggestive: Cefn-ddwysarn, Cors y Sarnau, and Sarnau – 'the ridge of two old tracks', 'the bog of the old tracks', and simply 'old tracks' respectively. It is such place name evidence that Waddelove points to in tracing many of the Roman roads (see Chapter Three).

This droveway could continue parallel to the modern road of the A494, keeping west of the later route and beneath Cefn Caer Eini and Caer Eini – or it could be consistent with a path some 4000 years older and take that route along the ridge. Both variations converge at Glan-yr-afon. To avoid an additional river crossing of Afon Alwen, the droveway would pass the river's confluence with the Dee upstream and then head east beneath Four Crosses and past the site of the Roman camp at Penrhos, looking out over the two river valleys. Here the route heads towards Cynwyd, passing Nant Rhyd-y-Saeson (the valley of the ford of the Englishman) and Tyn-y-Caeau to reach the crossing at Pont Dyfrdwy (SJ053413). This bridge is eighteenth century, with four spans in its passage over the Dee. Once on the east bank, a course to the north would take the route to Corwen, past Llan Garw Gwyn (Llangar Chapel – the church of the white stag).

An alternative route from Bala also departs from Cefn-ddwysarn (the second of the two old tracks on the ridge hinted at in the place name), heading through a low pass and descending to Llandderfel with its interesting church and contents and a nearby holy well after Derfel. This droveway heads east out of the village, closely hugging the western side of the Dee Valley. The Neolithic remains of Branas Uchaf tomb are to the east of the track, and further along the way at Tyfos, the Bronze Age cairn circle forms a large ring of boulders in another field right next to the west side of the road. This way joins the other variant route from Bala at Pont Dyfrdwy.

Toulson suggests a third possibility for this stretch, with a north-easterly departure from Llandderfel, over Mynydd Mynyllod by way of Garth-lwyd and Dol-drewyn. This path takes a curvilinear route across the east of its upper reaches, with a straight segment from Coed Gaerwen to Coed Pant Gruffydd, subsequently angling east and descending to join the first route from Bala below Penrhos.

Over the Berwyn Mountains

Droves from Corwen bypassing Llangollen on the way to Oswestry and Shrewsbury could take this route, heading south to Cynwyd first and then joining this eastern way to Bwlch Cynwyd on the Berwyn, keeping to the north of Afon Tristion and travelling ever further from the river. Having crossed near to the source of the Ceiriog Ddu, the way heads south between the rises of Cerrig-duon to the east and Cerrig Coediog to the west. After another crossing at Dolydd Ceiriog the way goes

Part of Toulson's proposed droveway from Bala to Corwen, not far from the Roman camp at Penrhos.

uphill to avoid a steep valley on the east, and then makes a jolting descent past Bronze Age burial cairns and eventually crossing the Nant Rhydwllym, a tributary of the Ceiriog. Here it is joined by the easterly route from Bala.

Bala to Llanarmon Dyffryn Ceiriog (for Oswestry and Shrewsbury)

The start of this route would use the lower droveway from Llandderfel, giving an easier passage to Llandrillo (Pont Fawr at SH982366 gives just as easy a crossing as the bridge further on, but has more inclines to go up and down before another ascent into the Berwyn). Having passed the ancient tomb at Branas Uchaf, there would be a south-easterly crossing of the Dee at Pont Cilan (SJ021375) – another eighteenth century construction with two spans. Passing through Llandrillo the route takes a course on to the hill of Moel Ty Uchaf, swinging around its northern contours capped with the Bronze Age ring cairn and other less impressive contemporaries to its south.

The way continues to the head of the Llandrillo Pass (Pen Bwlch Llandrillo) with Cadair Bronwen's imposing mass to the south. Following the Maids' Path the drove crosses the upper reaches of Nant Rhydwllym to end up on the northern reaches of Pen-yr-eryr, meeting with the droveway from Corwen and Cynwyd. The droveway then descends into the vale of Ceiriog, through Pentre and Llanarmon Dyffryn Ceiriog and climbing up again on a line projected through Rhiwlas, Llawnt and Oswestry. Such a route would be a reverse of the proposed prehistoric route mentioned in Chapter Two.

Is there also another droveway over the Berwyn? Literature at the beautiful waterfall of Pistyll Rhaeadr (described as 'taller than the Niagara Falls' from top to bottom and 'one of the wonders of Wales' – easily understood when confronted with the sight of the falls along the west of the lane

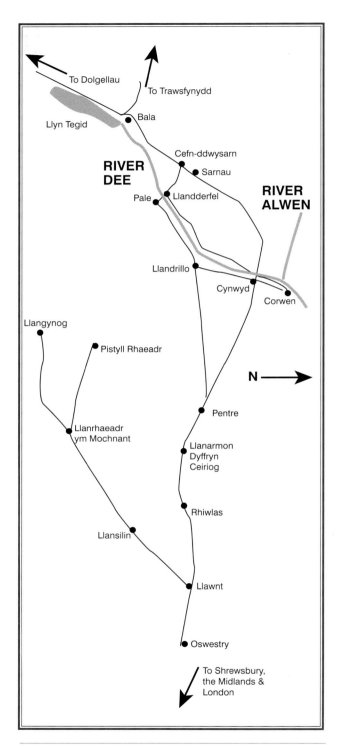

Map 4

from Llanrhaeadr ym Mochnant) mentions a drove route descending from the ridge of the Berwyn into the valley east of Nant y Llyn. Tracing where this route comes from is problematic, since if it travels from Bala the route would be needlessly prolonged if it came by way of Llandrillo and then into the wilderness, not to mention negotiating Moel Sych and Cadair Berwyn – the tallest ridge of the Berwyn. If taking a route that far north, it would be easier to travel a little further north on the Cynwyd to Pentre line.

There was much prehistoric activity in the moors and mountains above Pistyll Rhaeadr; the stone rows and circle of Rhos y Beddau, with a nearby almost hidden circle at Cwm Rhiwau and a spread of burial cairns (for the name means the moor of the graves), all show that there was much activity here BC, certainly generating prehistoric trackways. However, attempts to align them with their origins meet with uncertainty. The route to Pistyll Rhaeadr is similarly unclear, but the path onwards to Oswestry is clear enough, travelling through Efail-rhyd and Llansilin before joining the more northern Berwyn route at Llawnt and Rhydycroesau; or alternatively approaching via Croesau Bach.

In Llanrhaeadr ym Mochnant is an apparently re-used standing stone (SJ125259), with an inscription facing the road informing the traveller that Salop (Shrewsbury) is 26 miles distant, and London 180 miles; going by the 1770 date near the base one assumes that the stone was adapted to a new role in that year. A Latin inscription on the rear top face goes unnoticed and even less understood by those passing by.

Other prehistoric use of the area is attested by the Meusydd henge complex (SJ134252) across the road from

The standing stone-cum-milestone on entering Llanrhaeadr Ym Mochnant from the east.

Inscription on the eighteenth century milestone at Llanrhaeadr Ym Mochnant.

a modern coach depot, which once sat in the flat lush valley between the confluences of three rivers and has associated ring ditches and smaller circles which now only show as occasional cropmarks. Further on is the great hunk of stone named Post Goch (the red post) or Post y Gwiber (the post of the wyvern), among other variants. The name relates to legendary associations with a gwyber (a dragon) which was said to have been lured to its death on the stone. Its situation strongly suggests a marker in the expanse of the valley.

Bala to Welshpool via Dolgellau and Mallwyd (for Shrewsbury and Leebotwood)

As demonstrated by the toll road charges at the opening of this chapter, some droves headed south from Bala to Dolgellau to join those from Machynlleth. Some droves also headed northwards along the same route. The southward route seems an unlikely proposition given the amount of distance 'back west' it takes the droves, but nevertheless it was used. The route would have not been very different from the path of today's A494, heading down the west side of Llyn Tegid, crossing the still-young river Dee at Pont Rhyd-Sarn (the bridge of the old track river crossing) and passing a standing stone near Dolddeuli. Much of the route is parallel with, albeit at some distance from, the Roman Sarn Elen (see Chapter Three). If the drove entered Dolgellau then following the route to completion to rendezvous with other droves would naturally be required; otherwise the drovers would bypass the town and cross the Afon Wnion using some of the modern B4416 route, past Brithdir and taking a now-minor route across Braich-y-ceunant to Caerynwch, joining the main route to Dinas Mawddwy on the east of the Afon Clywedog. (16) With the existence of a later tollgate on leaving Dolgellau, this route would enable the drovers to bypass of one of the charges for using the road. With little opportunity for variation from the modern road, the way proceeds along the Bwlch Oerddrws with "…scenery so sublime as that among which Dinas Mawddwy nestles. For there is no place I think in all Wales quite so hemmed in by overshadowing hills." (17)

At Dinas Mawddwy, later home to another tollgate, this route arrives at the first of two significant bridges – Pont Minllyn (SH860139), a seventeenth century structure attributed to Dr John Davies of Mallwyd. Davies spent some 40 years between 1604 and 1644 as minister at St Tydecho's church in Mallwyd and has been referred to as one of the greatest of Welsh Scholars – though his enduring legacy for the trackways in the area were three bridges, two of which are essential to this route.

Pont Minllyn is a narrow twin-arched structure variably called a footbridge or a packhorse bridge, crossing over the Afon Dyfi adjacent to two later structures, the modern A470 road being the north-ernmost. If taking this crossing the droves could follow the way of the A470, then bend around to stay on the northern side of the Afon Cleifion to Cwm-Cewydd. A toll cottage is still visible a short way after leaving Mallwyd. The older track remains on the inside of the current road, converging at Pen-rhiwcul. Another possibility, lent weight by deep hollow ways, is that the route forded the Cleifion next to the dramatic single arch, hidden by the A470 road bridge which obstructs any easy view of the earlier seventeenth century structure just on its western side. Pont-y-Cleifion (SH86127) spans a narrow dark chasm and would indeed serve better as a packhorse way because of its construction (narrow width and allowing the animals to keep goods dry). A fording point is clear to the west of the chasm, with associated erosion and further hollow ways quite visible to indicate an entry into Mallwyd next to the roundabout. Alternatively, remaining on the west side of the Dyfi from Dinas Mawddwy and crossing below the confluence of the Cleifion at Pont Mallwyd (SH860122) is a possibility – this is the third of Davies' bridges, and of the three options, this one seems the least likely.

All of these routes converge at Pen-rhiwcul, with the latter two possibilities taking clearly visible older ways east of Mallwyd via Ysgubor Fawr and Colfryn. Striking eastward, the drove route cuts off the wider modern arc at Cwm Dugoed over the Afon Clywedog, with little or no opportunity for devia-tion from the modern route for many miles. Passing through Bwlch y Fedwen, the lower expanse of the valley either side of the Afon Banwy is marked by the occasional Bronze Age tumulus, one close to the droveway's crossing

Pont Minllyn at Dinas Mawddwy, a packhorse bridge following the droveway bound for Welshpool; one of the three bridges attributed to John Davies.

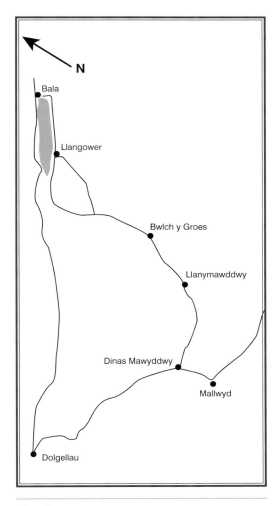

Map 5

Pont-y-Cleifion at Mallwyd; a dramatic single span packhorse bridge beneath the A470. Hollow ways from the river indicate a fording point west of the bridge.

at Pont Twrch. The route continues to Llangadfan, and the Afon Banwy is crossed before it passes St Cadfan's Well and reaches a fording point across the Afon Gam en route to Llanerfyl and Llanfair Caereinon (another toll gate here) by way of the B4385 to the south of the Banwy. Travelling on to Welshpool, either directly or via Berriew, the same B road route takes the drove on to Dolarddyn to join the course of the A458 (direct or south-east via Castle Caereinion for Berriew). That Welshpool received drovers is certain because of it being the largest town from Dolgellau to Shrewsbury, with the Dragon Inn accommodating drovers en route south and east.(18)

Welshpool to Shrewsbury/ Leebotwood

There seems much uncertainty and confusion as to what drove routes went which way; it is likely that different routes were used at different times and/or by different drovers, giving rise to difficulty in the sorting of possible routes. Working out the next stage of the eastbound or southbound route is helpful in tracing back the droveway within the region under examination.

Droves from Wrexham and Whitchurch would intersect at Shrewsbury, or alternatively could have departed east above Tong, along Ivetsey Bank through Norton Canes and Brownhills towards Northampton and East Anglia. (19).

Speaking of the relative importance of Shrewsbury and Chester for livestock throughput, Bradley remarks "…flannel and black cattle must have found their way into England in greater volume through this central market than by way of either the northern or southern extremity of the Marches." (20) The northern and north-western approaches seem certain, but what about those from the west exiting Wales and Welshpool?

If passing more or less due eastward toward

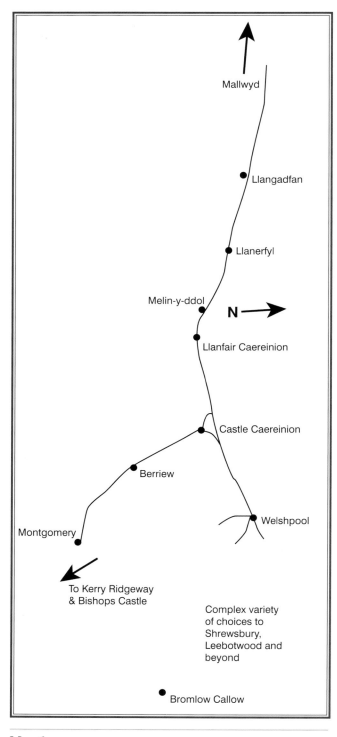

Mallwyd

Llangadfan

Llanerfyl

Melin-y-ddol

N →

Llanfair Caereinion

Castle Caereinion

Berriew

Montgomery

Welshpool

To Kerry Ridgeway
& Bishops Castle

Complex variety
of choices to
Shrewsbury,
Leebotwood and
beyond

Bromlow Callow

Map 6

Shrewsbury, the drove would pass the stunning hills of the Breidden with their the prehistoric settlements: "...the Breidden, looking veritably what in fact they are, two noble pillars of the chief gateway into mid-Wales." (21) The way leaves the principality just after Middletown; the route to Shrewsbury has very wide roads with established hedgerows set well back in places, with the original tracks to the south side being visible on occasion as they are bypassed by the A458. Come the turnpikes, a toll gate marked the exit from Welshpool to Shrewsbury.

Another Shrewsbury route leaves Welshpool on the east heading to Welsh Harp and a convergence of roads on the bend of Long Mountain. This route then follows the ridgeway through Vennington, Westbury, Yockleton, Nox and Cruckton towards Shrewsbury.

Bonser shows the drove routes from Oswestry and Llangollen approaching Shrewsbury from the north, without any western approach from Welshpool, or any course via Middletown. By inference, the Welshpool route would appear to loop south to Montgomery, utilising the ancient Kerry Ridgeway from Kerry to Bishops Castle, proceeding then by lanes above Lydbury North to Plowden. It then heads north across the ancient Portway over the Long Mynd, dropping to Church Stretton before heading north again through All Stretton to Leebotwood. At Leebotwood these droveways met the route south from Shrewsbury, converging on an eastward course towards Wednesbury. (22)

A piece of the puzzle here is directing the route so that it passes a prominent drove marker west of the

Scots Pine trees at Borth y Gest
– a significant marker for a drover.

Long Mynd. Which way did the droves head from here? A route could be cut to the south-east as the Bromlow Callow would be clearly visible. It is a recognised drove monument, but sending droves southward from Shrewsbury to this point would be nonsensical as the southerly exit from Shrewsbury avoids the uplands of the Long Mynd. It would be absurd to think of droves bound for London taking a substantial northbound diversion, adding on many miles and days to their trek, when the southern route along the Kerry Ridgeway and on via Plowden would suffice. This must surely be indicative of yet another route south-east from Welshpool to Leebotwood, via Black Marsh, Pennerley, north of the Stiperstones, through Bridges and heading through Ratlinghope to Woolstaston on a north-east route direct to Leebotwood. All the droves heading here would make for 'The Pound' inn, dating from at least 1650 with facilities for corralling the animals for refreshment and shoeing as well as hospitality for those driving them, before heading on to London.

There is considerable prehistoric activity in this area too; Mitchell's Fold and the Hoarstones stone circles are the survivors of a once-dense Bronze Age ritual landscape. Burial cairns and barrows mark the uplands and hilltops to the south and east for many miles. A route passing nearby Roundton Hill and the imposing Corndon Hill by the west side would also serve well as a drove route, with a wide path and hedges and trees indicative of droving. This is also the site of the Cwm Mawr or Hyssington Neolithic axe factory. Ancient routes passing through here are a certainty.

Borth y Gest to Harlech

Returning to the departure from the Lleyn Peninsula via the south-bound crossing, as noted above, prior to the construction of the Cob at Portmadog droves bound south-east for Harlech crossed the tidal sands of the Glaslyn estuary. At the time only a few houses existed at the (even now) small town of Borth y Gest. Reliance upon expert local knowledge for fording the tidal mouths of the rivers and the safest route across soft sand and mud was imperative. Getting it wrong would be disastrous. One can sit here and watch the tide inch up second by second with mesmerising effect. Should the tidal crossing be misjudged or attempted too late, it would be most unfortunate for any person or beast out on the flats with hasty evasive manoeuvres required.

One of the markers of a drove is purportedly a grouping of three Scots Pine trees. (23) Upon the western side of the harbour entrance at Borth y Gest are two clusters of these trees. These trees were generally planted as distinctive landmarks on the droveways, largely by farmers desirous of attracting attention and generating business, with the incidental formation of markers as a result. Living between 250 to 300 years, even surviving for over 500 years on rare occasions, the Scots Pines planted in the nineteenth century should be with us for at least another century if they survive to their fullness of time.

At this major crossing point, then, it comes as no surprise to find a significant droving landmark. As droving days were drawing to their close the tidal routes here became much busier with shipping as Borth y Gest blossomed into a major shipbuilding location with four boat yards in the harbour alone. The Ffestiniog Railway transported slate from the quarries in the area across the Cob to the quay at Porthmadog, from where the loads were taken by boat around the world. Borth y Gest's role in this industry dramatically enlarged the hamlet into a thriving village; the combined effect of these changes was to reduce the need for people to be guided across and traverse the estuary – perhaps bringing a tidal crossing to a close here. Earlier settlement is attested by a number of hut circles in woodland at Parc y Borth to the rear of the harbour. This may well have been a significant crossing point for a long time.

The point of destination is uncertain. There are in fact two river estuaries to cross here – the Glaslyn and the Dwyrd. Should the droves only follow the Glaslyn route, crossing to Trwynpenrhyn then continuing on above Portmeirion and Penryhndeudraeth, would give a circuitous detour via Maentwrog.

If the droves went across both estuaries, where did they aim at for their arrival on dry land? Unintentional uncertainty was not an option. The first consideration must be the lie of the sands and mudflats at the time. Sandbanks flow and change over time, and depending on winter storms and spring tides they will present themselves differently to subsequent travellers. The knowledge of local guides as to which ways were better for a given crossing would have been crucial. The shorter drove route bound for Harlech would have meant finding the best line for crossing the confluent Glaslyn and Dwyrd rivers. If the way veered too far to the east the marshes of Glastraeth would become a problem. The best landing place would have been between Llechollwyn and the three summits around Ogof Foel. These would serve well as landmarks for the drovers to aim at. Closer examination of the map does show a variety of tracks leading from the shore and curving southwards.

On to Harlech, the best way seems to be approaching from the north with the route from Ynys, heading to the rocky outcrop at Lasynys-Fawr and converging with the B4573 at Llechwedd-de-bach before entering the town to the east of the castle.

Harlech to Dolgellau

Exiting Harlech southwards on a road parallel to the B4573 and its convergence with the A496, the droveway heads to Llanfair, with the name of a settlement to the north-east, Muriau Gwyddelod, again recalling the Irish connection. Between Llanfair and Llanbedr the route is suggested by the name of the road –Sarn Hir, long old road.

Leaving Llanbedr from the east opposite the Victoria Inn, the droveway would begin its penetra-

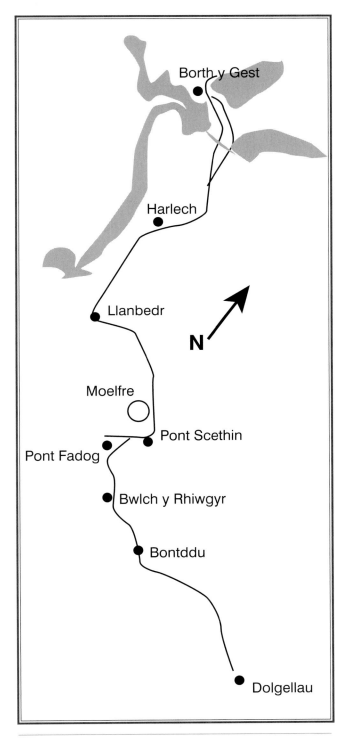

Map 7

tion of Cwm Nantcol, crossing to the Afon Cwmnantcol's southern side at a bridge of the same name. Sheepfolds and cattle grids dot the way and the landscape, in keeping with the route's agricultural past. Either side of Cil-cychwyn two ways lead into the mountains with a definite upward thrust, the first on course to Pont Scethin, passing between the rounded dome of a hill, Moelfre, and the wide Moelyblithcwm. A large number of prehistoric monuments and settlements, both visible and not so visible, dot the landscape to the south and west of Moelfre as well as further along the route.

On the way to Pont Scethin the route briefly converges with Waddelove's proposed Roman route from Dolgellau to the Porthmadog area, the two standing stones to the west of the bridge giving test to the ongoing passage of humanity in the area.

Crossing over the bridge the droveway heads south-west on the west side of Llyn Erddyn, taking an arc to avoid the worst of the ascending ridge on the south reaches of Llawlech. Joining localised drove routes from Dyffryn Ardudwy, the way swings with great certainty to the south-east with the pass of the Bwlch y Rhiwgr in sight. Those coming from Ardudwy would have passed a profusion of great megalithic monuments; they would also have passed Llety Loegr – an emergency shoeing station for cattle needing to be re-shod – and crossed over Pont Fadog, reminiscent of a fairy-glen. The converged routes have a variety of spectacular and diminished Neolithic and Bronze Age remains a short way to the south-west: stone circles, cairns, cairn circles, and the must-visit pair-

Looking up the droveway to Bwlch y Rhiwgyr, the notch in the hills, bound for Dolgellau.

Pont Fadog bridge a little further on from the shoeing station at Llety Loegr.

A last look home from Bwlch y Rhiwgyr towards Harlech and the Lleyn Peninsula.

Cadair Idris (centre) and the Mawddach estuary just visible to the right: a view to greet the droves heading for Dolgellau.

ing of chambers at Carneddau Hengwm stretching out parallel to each other on the mountainside. One of the chambers here even served as a hut at one point, with a hearth being installed in the cramped but cosy conditions.

Onwards and upwards, the drovers headed to the pass, a Bronze Age cairn intersected by a dry stone wall on the northern side, and may have turned for a last look back home towards Harlech as this staggering view gives way to the panorama of the Mawddach estuary and the sweeping heights of Cadair Idris to the south. Some way down the hillside, Cerrig Arthur stone circle sits at the junction of two old tracks showing the way to the pass over the Rhinogs; the droveway proceeds down to Bontddu and on to join the eastward march at Dolgellau.

Llangefni to Porthaethwy (Menai Bridge)

Daniel Defoe, of 'Robinson Crusoe' fame, wrote concerning Anglesey around 1685 that "it is a much pleasanter country than any part of N. Wales that we had yet seen, and particularly is very fruitful for corn and cattle," (24) and it is this ability to be able to supply other parts of Wales in times of shortage which contributes to Anglesey being suffixed as "The Mother of Wales".

The droves leaving central Anglesey, having gathered from the north, west and south at Llangefni from the outlying villages, fields and farms, would take the most direct route along what is now the B5429 through Ceint and Penmynydd to the biggest challenge for these northern drove routes – the crossing of the Menai Strait at Porthaethwy, now Menai Bridge.

Cattle had been sold from Anglesey to the mainland since at least the early 1400s. Four hundred years later the trade was still going on along an improved route courtesy of the Union with Ireland and Thomas Telford's ingenuity. In 1829–30 around 6,500 head of cattle are recorded as having left Anglesey. (25)

Crossing the Menai Strait

In the seventeenth century around 3,000 head of cattle swam the Menai every year. By the 1790s over 10,000 cattle a year had to brave the current across the Menai Strait. At low tide the animals would be driven onto Pig Island (Ynys Moch) which now supports the northern tower of Telford's bridge over the centre of the flow, and from there across to the Welsh mainland, leading to them being labelled as the "treasure galleons of Wales". Economic survival and prosperity rested upon these animals swimming safely and completing their journeys alive and healthy. One visitor records the spectacle, which must have been an amazing sight to see:

"…it fortunately happened that several herds of black cattle that had been reared in Anglesey were then crossing the strait, on their road to Abergelly fair… We were much amused with seeing a large herd driven over. They are urged in a body by loud shouting and blows into the water, and as they swim well and fast, usually make their way for the opposite shore. The whole troop proceeds pretty regularly till it arrives within an hundred and fifty yards of the landing place, where, meeting with a very rapid current formed by the tide, eddying and rushing with great violence between the rocks that encroach far into the channel, the herd is thrown into the utmost confusion. Some of the boldest and strongest push directly across and presently reach the land; the more timorous immediately turn around and endeavour to gain the place from which they set off; but the greater part, borne down by the force of the stream, are carried towards Beaumaris bay and frequently float to a great distance before they are able to reach the Caernarvonshire shore. To prevent accidents a number of boats well manned attend, who row after the stragglers to force them to join the main body; and if they are very obstinate, the boatmen throw ropes about their horns, and fairly tow them to the shore, which resounds with the loud bellowing of those that are landed and are shaking

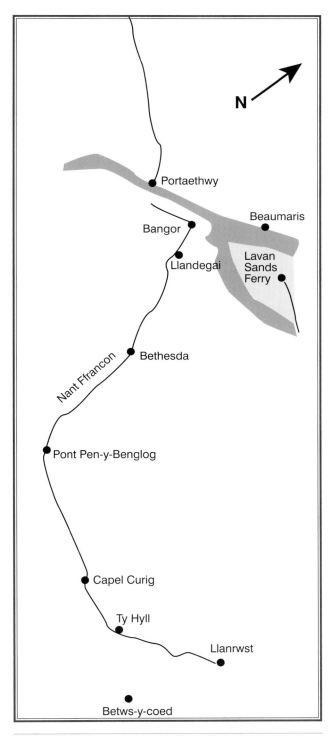

Map 8

their wet sides. Notwithstanding the great number of cattle that annually pass the strait, an instance seldom, if ever, occurs, of any being lost, though they are frequently carried to the very entrance of the Menai in Beaumaris bay." (26)

Bangor to Llanrwst via Capel Curig

To avoid the difficulties of getting several hundred livestock across the Penmaenmawr headland or taking them on to the risky tidal sands, followed by the impossibility of getting them across the Deganwy Ferry with the broad mouth of the Conwy gaping wide at that point, the line of the drove route takes a very large zigzag across this region to avoid the worst of the terrain, and also to coincide with many of the larger towns in the area.

Having left Bangor and Bethesda, the droves would then need to deal with the glacial cwm of Nant Francon. Given the narrow width of the bridge crossing of Pont Pen-y-benglog on the east side of the valley, the droves would have been better off taking the trackway on the west which avoids the narrow bridge. Even the Victorian traveller Bradley speaks of "the wintry horrors of Nant Ffrancon pass". (27) The way would then follow the south shore past Llyn Ogwen, beneath the Glyders to the south and the Carneddau to the north. The way on to Capel Curig would very likely have been along the axis of the earlier proposed Roman route and the later coach road, cutting an arc inside the curve of the A5 near the River Llugwy. To bypass the worst of the mountainous terrain, the droveway would then need to cut across north-east from Capel Curig towards Llanrwst.

The famous Ty Hyll or Ugly House,

Ynys Moch, centre, is the point from which cattle would be driven to swim the Menai Strait at low tide; the preparatory work for Telford's bridge levelled the craggy island to support the tower.

if its tradition is true, would have been an obvious waymarker for drovers passing through, as the way onward changes on its corner. It is told that the cottage was built by two rogue brothers in the fifteenth century who managed to perform a feat of construction overnight. Welsh custom dictated if someone were able to build their house between the hours of sunset and sunrise, with the fire going and smoke coming out of the chimney by the time dawn brightened the sky, the land would be theirs. If the age of this wonderful building is correct, it was passed by many droves taking this way to Llanrwst.

On the east side of Ty Hyll the drove route ascends north-easterly along the steep single-track lane, with twists and bends calling for precision driving and a lot of gear work for the motor vehicle. For those going on foot it would have been a far more pleasant but equally demanding ascent. The road passes several fantastic vistas, overlooking the Swallow Falls and Betws Y Coed area, disused mine workings, and significantly Llyn Sarnau –the lake of the old tracks. The steep descent towards Llanrwst requires very alert driving, and would have been hard work over its prolonged downhill jolt towards the historic bridge crossing at Llanrwst.

Llanrwst to Ruthin via Abergele

"The roads, except a good one from Abergele to Llanrwst, are indifferent and perpendicular," (28) remarked Bradley in 1905. Much of this road is based upon the earlier droveway, which departs Llanrwst from the north-east and then ascends the lower reaches of the northern end of the Cambrian mountains. The route takes the way of the A548, departing from this line south-east of Llangernyw; the village has an ancient church and a seventeenth century pub, the Old Stag, which could have caused a short detour if refreshment or accommodation were needed.

The church at Llangernyw has one of the oldest trees on earth according to some opinions; it is commonly dated to 4000 years old, making it a living Bronze Age yew tree, the oldest known tree in Wales, and listed as one of fifty great British trees by the Tree Council. The village takes its name from a fifth century Cornish saint, Cystenyn Gorneu, who had a son named Digain from whom the church takes its patronage. Two early Christian cross-incised stones are on the south side of the church, dating from the seventh to ninth centuries, and nearby there are two squat possibly prehistoric standing stones.

The drove would then proceed on to Llanfair Talhaiarn, heading north to Abergele along the course of the modern A548, intersecting the coach road en route and crossing the Afon Elwy. Abergele is the only other coastal stop for the droveways apart from Bangor. To arrive at Denbigh en route to Ruthin, the drove would need to leave Abergele at a steep south-easterly angle, taking St George's Road parallel to the current A55, heading up to Sarn Rug and on to Glascoed following the course of the Roman road (the modern B5381) for a short distance. A route to avoid later tolls would cut across Cefn Meiriadog via Sinan, passing the Neolithic chambered tomb at Ty'n-y Coed and descending once more into the Elwy Valley at Bont-newydd, below the caves once home to Wales' earliest known inhabitants. Taking the road curving through Coed y Trap it would be possible to follow a route to the north-east of Henllan then head down into the Vale of Clwyd at Denbigh.

On leaving Denbigh, the droveway would keep to the west side of the imposing castle via Pont Ystrad and Llanrhaeadr. Nearer to Ruthin, immediately preceded by a crossing of the Afon Clwyd, the droveway reaches Rhewl which literally means paved road. Here there is an eighteenth century building especially founded to cater for those droving the animals across the Vale of Clwyd: the Drovers Arms.

A droving inn has been on this site since at least the thirteenth century as demonstrated by the cellar, which easily predates the current structure. Infill between some of the beams consists of hazel wattle, with mud mixed with cattle hair to make the daub. The inn was probably paired with a farm at Rhyd y Cilgwyn, forming a symbiotic relationship. The farm was able to corral the animals and shoe them for their onward journey to Shrewsbury and London, and the drovers received refreshment and hospitality at the inn.

Ty Hyll –The Ugly House with the droveway to Llanrwst departing north-eastwards using the single-track road as it is now.

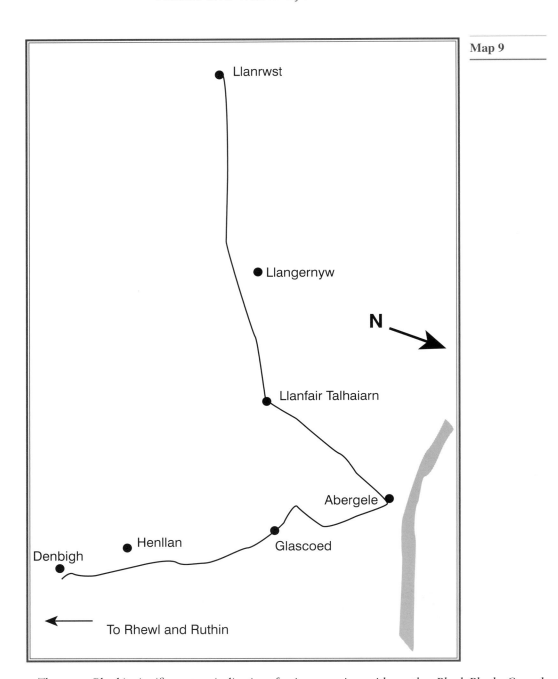

Map 9

The name Rhyd is significant too, indicative of a river crossing, with another Rhyd, Rhyd y Gwaed, forming part of the older drove route's passage before bridges were put in place. Droving at Rhewl was a deliberate target of the burgeoning of the railways in the 1850s, with a stop being constructed just 500 yards away to capitalise upon the money the herds would generate. Nevertheless, the drover Sylvanus Evans kept some of his livelihood going by undercutting the trains in his movement of livestock from Rhewl to Wrexham. Displays in the Drovers Arms show local drove routes from Rhewl across the ridge of the Clwydian Mountains to Cilcain (in the north-east) and Mold (to the north-east

The droveway from Ty Hyll to Llanrwst.

The Drovers Arms at Rhewl near Ruthin – still providing a warm welcome today

St Garmon's Church at Llanarmon Yn Ial, a meeting of many roads and and important point for droves heading to Wrexham.

Bwlch Oernant – The Horse Shoe Pass before 1925; used with permission (©) Judges of Hastings 01424 420919 www.judges.co.uk.

-east). The remainder of the route to Ruthin is best served by the path of the modern A525, which keeps to the manageably higher contours.

Ruthin to Wrexham via Llanarmon Yn Ial

Based upon the route suggested by Toulson from Ruthin onwards, the droveway departs along, and then onto Maes-y-Llan Road, heading south and briefly following the field boundary route of the B5429. Maintaining the eastward trend, it climbs between Moel Llanfair and Moel y Plas through a narrow prehistoric pass marked by round barrows. The descent takes the route to Llanarmon Yn Ial, with the conjunction of many roads and St Garmon's church central to the village. Llanarmon Yn Ial was able to serve the needs of the drovers very well; numerous smithies were located in the parish, with at least one dedicated to shoeing cattle; as the parish history booklet notes, "The area around Llanarmon was a big gathering ground for drovers." (29)

The direct route east from Llanarmon passes the large mound of Tomen y Faerdre, variously interpreted as a prehistoric 'goddess mound' or a castle. Whatever it was, it was recognised as the centre of the village before this shifted west with the focus upon the later church. Caves and another tumuli certainly add to evidence of pre-Roman activity in the area. Toulson proposes a toll-bypassing route which detours south of the village on the B5431 south-west of the church, joining the flow east at Graianrhyd. However, before charges were introduced the droves joined the modern B5430 to Graianrhyd on its south-eastward course through Rhydtalog, to Four Crosses, turning left for Bwlchgwyn where there was another opportunity to have cattle re-shod. The onward route from Bwlchgwyn is uncertain, but the descent to Wrexham would be best achieved by taking the Brymbo Road on to Tanyfron, or joining Old Road past Minera and Coedpoeth, with the possibility of linking with the extension of the recorded drove road near Plas-yn-fron.

Ruthin to Llangollen via Llandegla

The easier passage from Ruthin to Llandegla takes the course along a greater extent of the B5429 south to Graig-fechan, home to the Three Pigeons pub, once extended to improve its facilities for drovers. Bearing to the south-east on departing the village, the minor road leading beneath Moel Yr Acre and on to Pen-y-Stryt provides a straight-forward journey. An older way in and out of the village is visible from Court (SJ193518) past St Tecla's Well. Onward travel for Llangollen necessitates passage through the stunning Bwlch Oernant, better known in English as the Horse Shoe Pass – one of the clearest demonstrations of the topography of a landscape dictating the line of easiest passage. There are no alternatives for drove animals over Maesyrychen Mountain. A very steep descent to the east of the curvature of the pass is possible, but this would require a further ascent before arriving at Llangollen. The landscape is scarred by the quarries that have eaten away at the mountain tops, but the through route remains the same. Arrival at Llangollen is preceded by passing Eliseg's Pillar in the Valley of the Cross, and Valle Crucis Abbey further on. The scenes described by Borrow of the animals and traders at the cattle markets would be those to greet the droves as they arrived at this important stage of their trek to the fattening pastures and slaughterhouse.

CHAPTER 6

The Development of Roads and Trackways to Turnpikes and Telford

Following the Romans' departure, roads and trackways obviously continued in use but received little or no worthwhile attention for over a millennium. Edward I's Statute of Winton in 1285 ruled that 'no ditch, bush, or tree, capable of hiding a man, should be left within two hundred feet of any highway'; some report that this was put into effect between Chester and Rhuddlan (the latter being one of Edward's strategic sites) which would have cut a vast swathe across the landscape if it was enacted literally. – However, the road surface would only have received local repair insofar as was necessary to make the worst of the roads passable. From 1555 in the Tudor period through the reign of the Stuarts (to 1714), road maintenance was given over to the parishes, and the legal responsibility of the justices at their quarterly sessions oversaw this requirement. Resources, management, and variable amounts of will or apathy played their part in the continuing poor state of transport network. A road was seemingly not regarded as a structure requiring any care at all.

"…statutory repairs to it [the road] were usually undertaken in a purely agricultural spirit. The commonest method was simply to plough up the two edges of the track, throwing the earth inwards, and then level the surface with a harrow. A refinement consisted in filling up the ruts with stones or brushwood. Sometimes the whole surface was covered with gravel or broken stones; but this must have meant a good deal of heavy carting, and can only have been possible where carts were easily available. In general the process consisted in filling up the worst holes with something solid, and throwing back upon the surface the mud and gravel that the year's traffic had displaced." (1)

There were attempts under the Stuart government in 1618 to ease the damage to roads; they forbade loads greater than one ton in four-wheeled wagons. This was counter-productive as people loaded what should have gone as several four-wheeled wagons into two-wheeled carts instead – far more injurious to an unsurfaced road than any number of four-wheeled vehicles. The breadth of wheels was important in the efficacy of transport and the longevity of surfaces beneath them. A broader wheel was more sympathetic to the trackway, but likely to make harder work for the horses pulling them when passing over narrower ruts which were impossible to avoid. Wainwrights constructed wheels as narrow as possible, even though a proclamation in 1662 decreed that four inches should be the minimum wheel breadth for carts and wagons. If only all ineffective legislation was treated thus: the proclamation was withdrawn.

Something far more destructive was later devised to aid the progression of traffic but destroy even the most firm of surfaces. The wainwrights introduced protrusions to the wheel rims, often of bolt heads or nuts, which would stand an inch proud of the circumference. Whilst aiding the grip of the wheel in the stickiest of situations, the destruction to roads was considerable, eventually leading to turnpikes raising tolls for such wheels. Even the much later toll at Llanfairpwyllgwyngyll shows a double charge for vehicles with narrow or spiked wheels.

1663 saw the very first turnpike act come into effect in Hertfordshire; the legislation of 1555 placing care of the roads to the parishes was ineffective. Turnpikes were operated by means of Trusts that could only be formed by an act of Parliament. This enabled the Trusts to take measures necessary to look after the road, borrowing money against anticipated toll takings, appropriating resources such as gravel to make repairs when needed, as well as constructing the gates and tollhouses themselves. The name 'turnpike' comes from the pike which would be turned to open the gate adjacent to the tollhouse, allowing the paid-up traveller to proceed onward. In Wales these sometimes take the name of 'tyrpeg'.

The eighteenth century turnpike route to Croesor – comparatively passable compared to most routes of earlier years.

The idea was slow to catch on, but once it did the the turnpikes spread rapidly, with hundreds created during the eighteenth century. Between 1663 and 1700 there were five Turnpike Trusts created in England and Wales; by 1749, an additional 144 had been added to the tally. The next ten years up to 1759 added 171 turnpikes, with 170 more appearing in the decade up to 1769. 75 turnpikes were formed in the next ten years up to the end of 1779. (2) By 1770 the network was almost complete in North Wales.

The turnpike between Bala and Llangynog over the Berwyn was formed in 1769 largely for the transportation of corn from Llangynog. The first meeting of the trustees for this particular stretch was held on April 20th of that year, at the house of John Morris who is suffixed with the words 'the Goat'.

The toll is listed as:

Carriage and pair – Three pence

A cart load – Two pence

Horse or donkey – One pence

Twenty cattle – Ten pence

Twenty pigs, lambs or goats – Five pence

In later times the pike was operated by a couple, George and Mary, who received 'many pennies from travellers for their labour'; what must have been more of a gate than the usual pike was useful in preventing sheep from going astray.

Further north in the Clwydian range, the Parish of Llanarmon yn Ial had five toll gates within the parish: "One of these was at the Llanarmon road end, and was a big, square, stone building, which remained for a long time after it ceased to be used as a toll house. Another toll-gate was at Plas-yn-Cornel… There was also a toll house in Graianrhyd where two cottages, known as Nos. 1 and 2, Oldgate, stood until recently. They have now been converted into one modern house." (3) Even with such improvements, as late as 1905 come traveller's remarks such as this: "There is a wide enough choice of roads in the Vale of Clwyd, for it is threaded in every direction by byways that in dry weather are quite tolerable and well worth investigating, since they carry one through so many pleasant scenes, not only in Dyffryn Clwyd, but up towards Llandegla and the hills of Yale. In a wet season, however, it will be well to remark a poisonous mixture of clay and limestone detracts greatly from the joy, and even from the safety of

The toll at Llanfair, charging double for damaging wheels even in Telford's time.

one's progress." (4)

In the later part of the turnpike era, before railways took everything but local traffic until the arrival of the motorcar, two Scotsmen revolutionised the road network: J L Macadam, and Thomas Telford. Macadam's road business spread among a diaspora of family members who used much cheaper methods and materials than his competitor; though they took most of the North Wales turnpikes under their charge, it was Telford (see below) who was able to give the greatest lasting impact upon the communications routes through North Wales.

Another mode of transport rendered largely obsolete by the train revolution was the packhorse. These had their merits by being able to proceed in narrow lines through arduous terrain; on the other hand, they also had their demerits: "…on more tolerable roads there could be no doubt that they [horses] were the more economic means of transport; and even if the roads were bad, there was the overriding consideration that wagons were dryer and safer. If a packhorse gets bogged, the first thing to do is to relieve it of its load, and how that is to be done in a swampy place without wetting the contents of its pack may be a difficult problem. But if a wagon gets stuck in a slough, it may indeed require borrowed teams and a great deal of shouting to get it out again, but in the mean time the load will not be damaged if the slush does not rise above the axle tress." (5)

A packhorse trail runs through the Dolwyddelan Valley, south-west from Chester to Corwen, via Dodleston, Caergwrle, Ffrith and Bwlchgwyn. (6) At Caergwrle is a superb packhorse bridge, and further south there is Packsaddle Bridge near Pentre Bychan, Wrexham (SJ305477). A spectacular but unusable packhorse bridge, thought to be early mediaeval, survives under Telford's later bridge at Pont Pen-y-benglog. (7) A packhorse trail leads to Llanrwst from Capel Curig parallel to the drove route. A stepped trackway is noted at SH636486 east of Fedw-Bach on the ridge of Blaen Nanmor, above Llyn Dinas and Dinas Emrys in the heart of Snowdonia; this is also designated as a packhorse route. (8) The most famous of packhorse routes, though confusingly named, is the Roman Steps in the Rhinogs, crossing from Harlech to Trawsfynydd. The narrow steps are much more consistent with the passage of linear formations of animals than anything which the legions would have constructed.

Essential in the wider development of roads in North Wales was the Post Road to Holyhead. Originally running from Chester to Holyhead, the road may perhaps be summed up as "The Road to Hell" – not to equate Holyhead with the punitive afterlife destination, but referring to the nature of the road, described in 1688 by the following hellish endorsements: "I know not terms sufficiently expressive to describe this infernal road", with reference to a "heathenish country". (9)

The packhorse bridge at Caergwrle near Wrexham.

Post boys carrying mail first travelled the route on horseback in 1599 during the time of Elizabeth I. Seventy years later the route of the Royal Mail from Chester was recorded thanks to the monumental efforts of John Ogilby, born near Edinburgh in 1600, who in 1672 set about recording the major routes of England and Wales, later producing the first road map published in Europe. His story is compelling – although he lost everything in the Great Fire of London in 1666, fortune later saw him right. He was in the right place at the right time, and was charged with working out the ownership of land before the fire – a task which provided ample employment during the season of rebuilding. The proceeds from these labours enabled him to publish maps and atlases as well as other literature, and he passed away in 1676 having set England's and Wales' roads in print.

Following his maps on modern maps can prove difficult. The font and the variation in spelling are challenging. Many ways have changed in terms of their routes, landscapes, waymarkers etc. On the other hand, the old maps can provide vital information as to wayside markers of his time. It is his map of the Chester to Holyhead route which is described below.

Until Telford's A5 route gave an improved alternative, the London to Holyhead road entered Cheshire at Bridgemere, north of Woore, continuing on through Nantwich (with its London Road, Welsh Row and Welshman's Lane) and crossed the River Weaver. The post from Chester would depart from the south side of the city, taking Bridge Street and Lower Bridge Street. What is particularly noticeable about the map at this time is the width of the River Dee in relation to its proximity to Chester. It is much wider than it is today, and it was not until the much later silting-up of the Dee estuary and the rise of the port of Liverpool that Chester's access to the sea reduced.

The route then headed north-west to Bretton, having passed over a stone bridge. After Bretton it entered Wales and the Edwardian county of Flintshire, pushing on towards Hawarden. Passing through Northop on a westerly course and entering into Denbighshire, the approach to Denbigh enters the town along the same axis as the modern A543. Leaving Denbigh it then travels on to Henllan. The Llindir Inn is the only inn in the village, outliving any competitors and dating from 1229. The earliest part of the current structure probably dates to the late sixteenth century at the earliest, with many alterations added to its fabric since. (10) Henllan, as its name (meaning old enclosure) suggests, has a lengthy history with its church, across the road and uphill from the inn, founded by St Sadwrn in the sixth century, and a castle-like tower in the north of the churchyard dating from the eleventh century. The four corners of the tower are angled to point at the four cardinal points of the compass – a helpful navigational aid should those passing it be aware of such a geographically directive monument. Immediately to the east of the village is a Bronze Age tumulus – a round barrow, one of a handful in the area, indicative of earlier passage here.

The course then bears north-westward to Cefn Berain, avoiding an additional crossing of the Afon Aled, a tributary of the Elwy, which has its confluence with the larger river just beneath Mynydd Bodrochwyn (is this the 'Great Mountaine' marked on Ogilby's map?). Another link to the Irish connection occurs again in this area where the road crosses a bridge, Pont y Gywddel – the Irishman's Bridge. The coach road then follows the current B5381 to Betws-yn-Rhos (house of prayer in the moor), where the Wheatsheaf could provide a stopping point if needed. The church here is an 1838 construction upon the site of a previous church that dated from at least 1254 prior to its demolition for the new building. From Betws the road angles to the crossing at Deganwy, passing over Dolwen Bridge and then dropping down on to the east side of the Conwy into what was once Caernarvonshire. Sarn y Mynach, coming down to Glan Conwy Corner, was for a long time the approach to the ferry at Conwy; the ferry house stood on the north side of the road immediately across from the Castle, and thus began one of the (potential) hazards of the journey to Holyhead.

In 1189 there well may have been a ferry in operation on the Conwy, with the permission of Llywelyn the Great for monks from Aberconwy monastery in that year. Without heading further upstream,

The Llindir Inn at Henllan, on the old coach road from Chester.

options were very limited. The earliest date for another ferry is near Tal y Cafn in 1301 (it was not until 1897 that there was the first bridge crossing at Tal y Cafn); by 1429 ferries at Deganwy and Tal y Cafn become one operation on the two sites. The crossing even further upstream at Llanrwst was not built until 1636. A couple of fording points are hinted at by places names: Pen-Rhyd (SH793718) is near Tal-y-Cafn on the east side close to where Bodnant Garden is now, and Rhyd-y-Creua – the ford of the stepping stones – north of Betws y Coed on the east side (SH803571) is a considerable way south.

Accidents occurred while crossing here at Deganwy. The grave of such a victim in Llanrhos cemetery commemorates one of 13 who perished on Christmas Day 1806 when the ferry foundered. Besides the perils, the obstinacy of and the extortionate pricing imposed by the Deganwy ferrymen became widely reputed; people travelled instead to the Tal y Cafn crossing, or even further south to Llanrwst. From here the route in the later eighteenth century took the prehistoric and Roman way through the Bwlch y Ddeufaen thereby wholly avoiding the traumas of the Deganwy ferry and the Penmaenmawr headland. In 1777 the Caernarvonshire Turnpike Trust received the go-ahead from Parliament for a turnpike from Aber to the Bwlch y Ddeufaen. Ye Olde Bull Inn at Llanbedr y Cenin benefited from this diversion of traffic, but even though the route was used for a while, the attempt at turnpiking it proved too difficult, and other developments helped push the Great Irish Road from Chester further south via Betws y Coed (see below).

For now the route continues west having taken the Deganwy ferry and crossed to the west bank of the Conwy. There, three choices were available depending upon tides. If the tide was out, a northern route around the headland and along the shoreline could be taken. Given the right conditions it

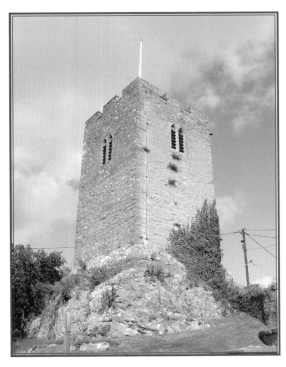

The tower in the churchyard at Henllan, aligned with its corners on the cardinal compass points.

was then possible to continue on to the Lavan Sands ferry on the tidal flats opposite Beaumaris; however, timing was of the essence for the health and safety of all concerned. If it was foggy the exact point of the ferry departure could be invisible, and there were obvious perils in the cloaking of the way forward. If the tide was in then it would be necessary to take the route via the Sychnant Pass running to the south; this name literally means 'dry valley', as opposed to the wetter alternative route to the north.

Coming into Dwygyfylchi and Penmaenmawr, most would pray that the tide would

The Wheatsheaf and St Michael's Church at Bettws yn Rhos en route from Chester on the post road.

be out to avoid the second hazard of this route: taking the trail over the headland between mountain and precipitous drop into the waves beneath. Today's headland at Penmaenmawr is still impressive, though the use of cars and the modern road through the relatively recent tunnel somewhat anaesthetises one to the awe of nature and the sense of travel through a landscape with all the perils, hazards, sights, sounds, smells and experiences it can offer. Misleading as this is, in cars people feel safest of all when compared to the forms of transport that went before them. This headland has been substantially reduced; there was once a hillfort on it, but like most of the mountain it has been quarried into oblivion, reducing the awe that must have struck those traversing its northern flanks. Several accounts of this part of the passage along the North Wales coast survive today.

Giraldus Cambrensis in 1188 wrote concerning his eastward route through North Wales: "We then continued our journey along the coast, with the sea on one side and a steep cliff on the other, until we came to the River Conway…" (11) Bradley in 1905 writes with the benefit of a more pleasant crossing of the headland, reflecting upon those who had gone before: "'A narrow pathway for passengers,' says Camden, 'rocks hanging over one above and the raging sea beneath.' Sir John Branston, writing in 1631, tells us he had to 'lift his wife over the back of the saddle for her fright.' This was the only road to Holyhead at that time, and the Lord Lieutenant of Ireland in the next century approved a scheme for making it 'nowhere less than four feet wide, and at present too well known for its deep and dangerous passage.' By 1770 they had achieved a road seven feet wide, and protected in the worst places by a wall one foot high! At last the nerves of Irish travellers could stand it no longer, and the city of Dublin subscribed sufficient to make a wall breast high between passengers and the yawning abyss below, for the present road is much lower down than this awesome horse-path on which our forefathers travelled." (12)

As a third option after disembarking from the Deganwy ferry, a route continued on land to Bangor where one could use the services of one of the Menai ferries at Porthaethwy for Anglesey. In the seventeenth century the ferries were small and oval in shape, carrying a load of three horses comfortably, though later designs were able to take carriages onboard for the perilous crossing.

There had been a ferry in operation at Porthaethwy since before Llywelyn the Great's victory in battle in 1194, described as "the passage of the Menai at Porthaethwy". It has always been the narrowest part of the channel, and therefore the most obvious point for a ferry, landing between the islands of Pig Island (Ynys y Moch) and half tide island and serving as an easier passage when the tides were right. In 1686 a licence was granted for the construction of a house on Porthaethwy Common especially to accommodate ferrymen. Named "The Three Tuns", it was much better known as the Cambria. Traffic here increased dramatically with fairs being held on land situated behind the Cambria, as well as fairs across the water on the Bangor side at Treborth. The Cambrian route was further east than the suspension bridge that later replaced the path. This was a more east–west

crossing, landing very close to the Cambria and serving fairs held to its rear. A further ferry route known as Craig yr Halen existed to the west of Telford's masterpiece, crossing parallel to the later bridge.

Ecclesiastical authorities had their own private ferry route sailing between Gorad Road and Cadnant; this would have been the way taken by

The Inn at Tal y Cafn – a crossing of the Conwy since at least 1301.

The Sychnant Pass looking west; road to the left.

The Sychnant Pass looking east, before 1925; used with permission (©) Judges of Hastings 01424 420919 www.judges.co.uk.

Giraldus Cambrensis to preach on the Anglesey shore of the Menai, attempting to recruit more people for the Crusade from the likes of Rhodri ap Owain Gwynedd and his band of followers.

If one were able to use the Lavan Sands ferry, one would land just outside the south-west tip of the town; the coach road continued westwards along the same route as the modern B5109, but then diverged through Llansadwrn, Pen-y-garnedd and Rhoscefnhir. North of Ceint it turned south-west and then headed west to Llangefni – upon the same route as was probably utilised by the

The Penmaenmawr Headland as experienced by travellers today.

Romans in their avoidance of the marsh either side of the Afon Cefni. The coach route continues on through Bodffordd, Llnyfaes, Trefor, Bodedern and Llanynghenedl, then turns south-west towards Valley. Just north-east of Bodedern is a pair of dolmens (SH348809) – an arrangement which happens not infrequently in Gwynedd and Anglesey – and just to their south-east is a Bronze Age round barrow (marked tumulus) with a small standing stone in the fields of Shop Farm facing the road just above Llanynghenedl. Perhaps this coach road lies on or close to the course of an older route across the island (see Chapter Two).

Three possibilities were again presented here, two of them subject to tidal conditions. One option took a route across the sands when the tide was low to Cleveock Sands; a second crossed 'rocks and sand' on a course apparently similar to Telford's Stanley Embankment; and the third option for a dry crossing taking a more circuitous route via Four Mile Bridge, so-called as it is four miles south of Holyhead. This would follow a road through Trearddur, arriving at the destination approximately 20 hours after leaving Chester if luck was in their favour; if not, it could take up to three days.

In 1809 the Eagle and Child Inn at Holyhead advertised coaches setting out with the Royal Mail to London "By way of Chester, every morning, in 48 hours", with fares inside the coach priced at £6 and 6 shillings (half price for outside). Travellers only going as far as Chester paid £2 and 5 shillings. Alternatively, coaches departed from the Antient (sic) Briton each Sunday, Tuesday, and Friday morning, , travelling by way of Shrewsbury and heading for the Bull and Mouth in London; inside fare £4 and 4 shillings, outside £2 and 10 shillings. Travelling to Salop (Shrewsbury) only cost a mere £1 and 15 shillings inside, and ten shillings less outside at £1 and 5 shillings. The Prince of Wales Post Coach, each Monday, Wednesday, Thursday and Saturday to Shrewsbury cost the same. However, there is the clause that "The proprietors of the above coaches will not be accountable for any parcels above the value of £5, unless entered and paid for accordingly."

Besides the main Post Road through to Holyhead, by 1710 mail ran from Chester to St Asaph, and by the 1790s a network of services was in place, whch operated for fifty years from Chester through market towns such as Bala, Beaumaris, Caernarfon, Pwllheli and Welshpool. It was the post that was to be key in the development of through routes in North Wales. Even by 1770 a person recently arrived at Holyhead spoke of their horses having 'sunk into the clay' journeying from Beaumaris, even though the road from Porthaethwy to Holyhead was turnpiked in 1765.

By the eighteenth century improvements to the still terrifying but no longer quite so petrifying crossing of the Penmaenmawr headland afforded greater convenience for Irish traffic; consequently the Lavan Sands ferry began to fall out of favour with the Porthaethwy Ferry taking precedence for wheeled traffic after the 1720s. A dedicated inn was constructed called Cae'r Glowr, which was en- larged in 1777 and renamed with more English- friendly name of The George. Its own ferry route to Porthaethwy, which landed at Porth y Wrach, a little inlet to the north-east of the Cambria, was used for the next fifty years.

The need to get the Holyhead Road sorted once and for all became imperative against the back- ground of political unease over Ireland, the French incursion into Fishguard in Pemrokeshire in February 1797, and rumours of a Napoleonic invasion (or at least rumours of rumours). Communi- cation between London and Dublin had to be improved, and this road was the one big hindrance. Wider political developments affected the choices which were made.

Ferrymen seem to have had a bad reputation everywhere, on the evidence of similar complaints to those made about the Deganwy crossing at Conwy. Concerning the Porthaethwy ferries, 1782 saw a meeting at Gwyndy on Anglesey of the Isle's 'gentlemen' to hear out complaints ranging from excessive pricing, the perilous condition of the ferry boats, and unnecessary delays. This contributed to the weight of debate that would lead to Thomas Telford's bridge plans. By the time of the Act of Union in 1801 two public coaches (on average) were crossing to Ynys Mon each day.

To further his prosperity, in 1791 Lord Penrhyn built a road from his quarries at Bethesda northwards to Llandegai and Port Penrhyn, and south-eastwards along the west side of Nant Francon to Capel Curig and then on to Pentrefoelas. This had the unintentional but eminently sensible consequence of sending the Great Irish Road and Royal Mail along an entirely different route. So Penrhyn's 1790 road construction through Capel Curig enabled the Royal Mail to be moved in 1808 from the haz- ardous northerly coastal route to make use of the improved roads around Capel Curig and avoid the ferries at Deganwy. Local mail continued to utilise the former coach road from Chester, but the Holyhead mail now went along this, the 'Great Irish Road'.

The way from Llandegai to Pentrefoelas was turnpiked in 1802 along with another road up Nant Francon, this time on the east side over Pont Penybenglog; however, there were still problems. Pont Cyfyng at Capel Curig was a helpful solution for the coach road through the gorge past the Swallow Falls, but the route as a whole remained inadequate as coaches could not pass each other further on. To the south-east, the route near Penmachno was likened in 1809 to a staircase that had replaced a ladder; in that same year there were six incidents involving the coach overturning or sustaining structural failure through the demand of the 'surface' placed upon it by the road (13). On Anglesey in 1808 during an attempt to extend the mail coaches' route to Holyhead, one week saw three horses pulling the services stumble on the surface, breaking their legs as a result. Seven Turnpike Trusts operated the roads between Shrewsbury and Holyhead, with the common feeling being that the further west one went, the worse the road became. Uniform ease of passage was imperative.

Thomas Telford, 'The Father of Civil Engineering', seemed an unlikely hero of his later field judging from his origins as the son of a shepherd. Born in a small cottage next to Megget Water in Glendinning in Dumfrieshire on 9th August 1757, he went on to become an expert and renowned stonemason by 26 years of age and subsequently gained commissions as an architect. Receiving the appointment of the Surveyor of Public Works in Shropshire gave him direction towards overseeing the construction of a wide range of all things pertaining to transport across Britain. Given the quality of his architecture, his deep esteem for the benefits of experience, the value he placed on knowledge of the materials to be used in construction, and his emphasis on the good working practice of his men, he garnered respect from all quarters. He gained great loyalty from his workforce, with a team

The London–Holyhead coach at Tyn-y-coed.

of craftsmen and engineers 'sans pareil' who would accompany him over different projects. In 1810 Parliament impressed its commission on Telford, to find the best route across North Wales, including Anglesey, and suggest a means of bridging the Menai Strait.

At the instigation of the Holyhead Road Commission in 1815, Telford instructed three of his team to survey the entirety of the route from London to Holyhead, with the addition of the road from Chester to Bangor since the mail from Liverpool and Manchester took this route to join the journey to Holyhead. Starting in September 1815, the team completed their appraisal in March 1817. Some of the report must have been fed back in advance of entire completion, because parts of the infrastructure were embarked upon straight away. The single most dramatic piece of the work was that which completed the route in 1826.

Telford's bridge across the Menai Strait was not the first structure to link Anglesey with the Welsh mainland. In September 1277, Edward I's forces under Luke de Tany constructed a bridge by tethering ships together, with the materials and workforce supplied by boat from Rhuddlan. Unlike the Romans 1200 years before who sought to conquer Anglesey from the mainland, the strategy in this case was to use the granary of Anglesey as the base from which to launch attacks on Snowdonia.

"Shortly after the English arrived on the island, there was a frenetic outburst of activity at Rhuddlan as vast amounts of supplies were made ready for onward shipment to Anglesey so that work on the construction of the bridge could commence. Quantities of building materials, timber, iron and nails were purchased, as well as more substantial items such as boats. Carpenters were over to put the bridge together. The fleet played a vital part in the operation, shipping supplies and men across the seas where they were immune from attack by the Welsh… By the end of September the bridge was completed". (14)

A number of options for providing a crossing before Telford's had been explored, but none had been satisfactory. Bridges of stone or timber or an embankment at Swilley Rocks (Ynys Geint, south-west from Pig Island) both were considered, but given that over 4,000 ships used the Menai Strait annually at that time, neither of these proposals provided what was needed. In 1810 Thomas Telford began his deliberations following the commission from Parliament, later coming to rest upon two particular favourite crossings for bridges; in Telford's own words, characteristic of the time,

"The duty assigned me being to consider and report respecting a bridge across the Menai I shall confine myself to this object. Admitting the importance of the communication to justify acting on a large scale I not only consider the constructing of a bridge practicable but that two situations are remarkably favour-

Lord Penrhyn's track looking up Nant Ffrancon; the turnpike and Telford's road visible as a line on the left.

able. It is scarcely necessary to observe that one of these situations is at the Swilley rocks and the other at Ynys y Moch. These two being so evidently the best the only question that can arise is to which of them preference ought to be given ...". The latter option was the most favourable: "...From leaving the whole channel unimpeded it is certainly the most perfect scheme of passing the Menai and it would in my opinion be attended with the least inconvenience and risk in the execution." (15)

The new bridge obviously brought great changes for everyone concerned with what was to become Menai Bridge, with changes to the layout of the settlement as it was amended to aid the flow and construction of the new road and dry crossing. New roads were constructed over Cerrig Y Borth for Holyhead. Other streets such as Dale Street and the seemingly self-aggrandising Telford Road were made to join with the older curvilinear coastal route, forming a triangle with the Holyhead Road to the west.

The new embankment, essential to give the Holyhead Road its necessary elevation to join with the bridge surface at a height sufficient to allow clipper ships to pass underneath, obstructed the route between Craig yr Halen and the Cambria. This route was subsequently altered to pass under the first arch of the bridge, to allow connection between the older points of communication.

With all the labour for the bridge local lodgings were in high demand, and new buildings sprang up early in the construction in 1818, as other preparatory efforts were undertaken and the project

The Menai Bridge – the south tower.

began to gain momentum. Carpenters and smiths were engaged and all manner of auxiliary buildings were built and brought into use, with 200 men working on the project in the local area alone.

"Pig Island" was flattened somewhat to allow the bridge tower to be built upon it using cranes, essential to the towering structure coming into being. Further quays were constructed to allow materials, including stone quarried at Penmon on the east tip of Anglesey, to be brought in by sea. On 10th August 1819, the day after Telford's birthday, the first stone was laid; by March 1821 the supports, or piers, were 60 feet high. By July 1823 they were at road height with much of the remaining structure either ready for installation or in an advanced state of completion.

The Menai Bridge has impressive statistics. The height of the carriageway is 100 feet above high tide mark, with a total height of 150 feet. Its complete span is 1500 feet with 580 feet of this distance being suspended. There are 16 chains, each weighing 23 tons, which were produced at Ironbridge in Shropshire by one ironmaster Hazeldine, –illustrating Ironbridge's place in cutting-edge technology of the time. It was the raising of the chains that was the most perilous and arduous part of the construction, but to everyone's satisfaction and safety this mercifully passed off successfully in the summer of 1825, beginning on Tuesday April 26th. After a perfect morning and with the approaching high tide the 450-foot-long chain, spread out on a raft, was manoeuvred into place by four boats. The central part of the chain was then secured to each end of the land-held chain; 150 men on the Anglesey side then began rotating capstans with the accompaniment of a band to aid in the winching. Upon completion of this first chain's lifting into place there was much jubilation amongst the workers and massed spectators who had been gripped by the scene. As Telford was one who rewarded the efforts of his labourers, this risky part of the construction of the road to Holyhead and London was marked "…with plenty of ale and substantial accompaniments… in the disposal of which the men showed the same active zeal which had marked their previous conduct".

Each nine-foot chain link was forged at Upton Magna east of Shrewsbury and transported by canal to Shrewsbury for tensile tests. Here they were heated up and bathed in linseed oil (not wine, as suggested by Lewis Carroll in "Through the Looking Glass") to defend them against the saline environment. Then they were taken to Weston Lullingfields and Chester by canal, and finally by sea to the Menai Strait. The first chain took two hours twenty minutes to lift into place; by the time the sixteenth chain was in place on 16th July the process had been refined to a mere 90 minutes.

30th January 1826 saw the bridge open, to celebrations far and wide; flags were even flown from the Pyramids in Egypt, and a decent meal with plenty of good ale was brought in to mark the occasion for all those who had worked on the project. It had taken nearly 50 years from initial discussions and arguments in the 1780s for the bridge to be realised. Robin Ddu, a sixteenth century poet, had spoken prophetically of the Menai Strait being bridged in the future. Certainly the bridging must have been something that had crossed people's minds for millennia beforehand, in times when all that was lacking was the technology to literally bridge the expanse.

Aside from the bridge, the wider aspect of the road from Shrewsbury was similarly auspicious in its endeavours. The Welsh side of the project was "not so much a matter of road improvement as of road making". (16) Telford's road construction technique was not only modelled upon the Romans', but the Roman method was expressly cited in his own articulation. Material was graded, with larger stones forming the foundation layer (after the surface had been levelled and drained) followed by a further layer of stones 'the size of walnuts', and then (if available) a non-essential thin layer of gravel was placed on top. Where he was able to make use of straight lines, the most obvious way of traversing a landscape since humans first analysed such issues, Telford did so. The A5 at Cerrigydrudion has been mistaken for a Roman route by at least one important book on prehistory. (17) Unlike any of his predecessors, Telford made provision for roadside storage depots so that ready-graded material could be at hand for road repairs as needed.

Once the Commission had the amassed the finances, work could begin, and the seven Turnpike Trusts could be bought out to bring the desired uniformity of condition to the road. Telford's management of the project was nothing short of commendable. The meticulous surveying undertaken prior to the go-ahead paid off. Instead of starting work on a linear A to B route, his superlative planning took a different approach. He undertook first of all to improve the stretches of the route most in need of action. The work was effected so that the improvements to the roads could be brought into action at the earliest possible time. Coaches were able to reach Bangor by 1819 – not only benefiting the road users, but serving as good publicity for the work already complete and that still to be done, as well providing as proof (if any were needed) that Telford had the job in hand.

The Menai Bridge – still awe-inspiring after 180 years of service.

One of the earliest pieces of work must have been the Waterloo Bridge at Betws y Coed, for which the arch was constructed in 1815 (as celebrated in the text on the side of the bridge, missed by nearly all road users nowadays and viewable only via a conscious effort to do so). The road was not in place that year, contrary to popular misconception. The arch was not delivered to Betws y Coed until at least 1816. The design includes aspects of the four nations now united into a Britain that, as demonstrated by Napoleonic defeat at Waterloo, was a Great Britain. The features incorporated are a rose, shamrock, leek and thistle. (18)

An embankment at Chirk eased the gradient towards Llangollen, as did the Ty Nant embankment well west of Corwen; an early improvement from Dinas Hill to Rhydllanfair near Pentrefoelas addressed one of the worst stretches. More improvements were made to the gradient of the road west of Swallow Falls, and a new bridge, Pont Ty Hyll and another embankment took the route to the higher ground above the turnpike to Pont Cyfyng (now the minor route past the site of the Roman fort of Caer Llugwy).

The rock at the neck of the Ogwen Valley and Nant Ffrancon was blasted through, enabling the creation of an embankment on the earlier turnpike route and creating a wider terrace with a retaining wall upon the road's west side on the almost sheer sides as the road approached Bethesda. Another impressive part of the undertaking was the Stanley Embankment, giving a dry passage to Holyhead and avoiding a detour via Four Mile Bridge. It was opened in 1823, being 1,300 yards long, 16 feet high, 114 feet at its base and 34 feet at the top, having taken a year to a construct by Telford's contractors. (19)

Besides the Shrewsbury to Bangor section there was also the North Wales Coast Route and the bridging of the Conwy, which Telford completed with a sympathetic 'harmonious composition' incorporating crenellations on the bridge towers, echoing the imposing presence of Conwy Castle

Reaching into the distance – Telford's A5 at Cerrigydrudion.

across the water. This was another important work: "The committee of the House of Commons appointed to inquire into the state of the Chester and Holyhead road, found that great delays occurred in the arrival of the mails from Chester at Holyhead, which were owing partly to the bad state of the roads, but in a still greater measure to the ferry at Conway which was attended with serious inconvenience, much delay, occasional danger, and even actual loss of lives…The road way of the bridge is suspended from cables, similar to the Menai, carried over towers at the points of suspension. Here, however, there is only one roadway, with foot paths on each side…The pillars supporting the cables are about twenty four feet high from the road way, and the distance from high water mark to the road way is about eighteen feet. The depth of water under the bridge at high water is generally from twenty three to twenty six feet, and at low water from twelve to fifteen feet." (20)

At the completion of the Conwy bridge in July 1826 there was again celebration and much interest, although Telford was intentionally absent. He turned 70 just over a year later. His construction underwent some demanding tests courtesy of the weather within its first 13 years. In January 1836 a gale generated a vertical shaking in the bridge of some 16 feet, and in January 1839 hurricane-force winds shook the bridge so violently that the deck was impassable with sections hanging above the water; the bridge keeper was forced to use a boat to travel to the Bangor side, narrowly preventing a London mail coach from falling to a watery grave. (21)

Innovation continued to be the name of the game for road technology in North Wales. The bridge further to the west of the Menai Bridge was the product of Robert Stephenson, who had come up with the idea of a 'tunnel in the sky' for trains to pass through on the Chester to Holyhead route which he had been constructing. This train bridge opened in 1850. As part of the communications with Ireland the vast breakwater at Holyhead was finished in 1873, and the Menai Bridge received its covering of tar in 1896.

In 1922 weight restrictions were brought in to ease the burden on the bridge. Anything over four and a half tons was barred, vehicles were to travel at least 50 feet apart from each other and the speed limit was lowered to four miles an hour. The life of the bridge has continued since, with some strengthening of the carriageway and renewing and realignment of the vast chains between 1938 and 1941. This was carried out by Messrs Dorman Long and Company of Middlesborough, who undertook the challenge of allowing the bridge to remain in use while the deck was renewed – there was no other road route into Anglesey until May 1980, when the Britannia Bridge received its car deck above the train passage following a devastating fire in 1970. The method used to renew Britannia was to construct the new road deck beneath the older surface, and then raise it into place after the old deck had been dismantled.

All this served the increasing pace of automated transport as the rise of the car continued well into the twentieth century. The Menai Bridge required a toll, although this was lifted after prolonged calls for its abolition beginning in 1934 with protests from a host of councillors, Chambers of Commerce

The River Conwy viewed from the Waterloo Bridge.

across the region, and the likes of Mr Lloyd George and Miss Megan Lloyd George. Even so, tolls remained in place as of 1st April 1935; no April Fool, there were charges for motor and horse-drawn vehicles. A sign records the charges for a daily toll and a quarterly season tickets; the first figure applies to the daily charge, and the second to the quarterly charge where relevant:

Menai Suspension Bridge.

Schedule of Tolls.

1st April 1935.

Mechanically Propelled Vehicles.

For Every

Public Service Vehicle adapted to seat eight or more Passengers. 1s. 3d.

Other Hackney Vehicle. 3d.

Goods Vehicle Taxed as Goods (Agricultural). 3d. 2s 6d.

Other Goods Vehicle. 6d. 5s.

Trailer Drawn by a Goods Vehicle Other Than A Goods Vehicle other than a Good Vehicle Taxed as Goods (Agricultural). 6d.

Motor Car of Classes not specified above. 6d. 5d.

Motor Cycle with or without a Side Car and for every Motor Tricycle. 3d. 2s 6d.

Tractor Taxed as Tractor (Agricultural). 3d. 2s 6d.

Other Tractor. 6d. 5s.

Trailer drawn by a Tractor other than a Tractor Taxed as Tractor (Agricultural). 6d.

Horse-Drawn Vehicles.

For Every

Cart, Carriage or other such vehicle having:–

Four Wheels and Drawn by more than Two Horses. 1s 3d.

Four Wheels and Drawn by Not more than Two Horses 6d. 5s.

Two Wheels. 3d. 2s 6d.

More than Two Wheels and Used for Agricultural Purposes. 3d. 2s 6d.

The following qualifications are offered:

"No more than one toll is demanded in respect of the same vehicle for passing and repassing any number of times on the same day to be computed from 1am to 1am provided that for any vehicle by which passengers shall be conveyed for hire, toll shall be paid for each time of passing and repassing.

Season tickets are not available in respect of any vehicle carrying passengers for hire." (NOTE in the Oriel Ynys Mon in Llangefni, Anglesey)

Pont Cyfyng serving the older turnpike route, replaced by Telford's bridge at Ty Hyll.

The A5 through the Ogwen Valley.

Looking north down Nant Ffrancon – Telford's road built upon the earlier turnpike.

Pont Pen-y-benglog between the Ogwen Valley and Nant Ffrancon pre 1925; Postcard in author's collection, copyright holder and publisher not identifiable.

The typical octagonal Telford-designed turnpike house at Llanfair.

The Stanley Embankment looking east near Holyhead, and a Telford-designed milepost.

A commemorative stone presented by the Institution of Civil Engineers – Wales, marking the anniversary of Telford's 250th birthday.

Such toll designations may seem Pythonesque by today's reckoning, but nevertheless they proved a heavy tax, on locals particularly, and were eventually abolished. On the approach to Menai Bridge now stands a memorial to commemorate this gargantuan masterpiece of architectural beauty and innovation. The Institute of Civil Engineers had it placed in 2007 to mark the 250th anniversary of Telford's birth (a similar monument also exists on the west end of the Stanley Embankment). Telford was the Institute's first president during the construction of the Menai Bridge in 1820. Telford passed away on 2nd September 1834, leaving an exemplary legacy of constructions and routes across Britain that has never been equalled as the product of one person's intellect and creativity either before or since.

Shortly after the death of Telford, between 1839 and 1844 South and Mid-Wales were rocked by the Rebecca Riots. These were so called because men dressed themselves as women called Rebecca and possessed the toll gates of those they saw as forcing high taxes upon road users. Their inspiration came from Genesis 24:60: "And they blessed Rebekah and said to her, 'Our sister, may you increase to thousands upon thousands; may your offspring possess the gates of their enemies.'" (22) The violence and protests never spread further north than Rhayader, but later the 1880s saw the Tithe Wars in the north of the principality. Though this unrest concerned payments due to the clergy, it was very much seen as a continuation of the 'spirit of Rebecca' shown against the toll gates and houses 50 years earlier.

The road continues in use today; it is noted that "There is only one good road, the A5, which tears through the centre of the island to Holyhead and the ferry to Ireland. The traffic using it never stops." (23) Unthinkable as it would have been in Telford's day, sections of the A5 are have already been rendered obsolete, receiving additions or even being bypassed in numerous locations. Work west of Corwen bridge is a result of the continuing the trend of road engorgement, with through-routes no longer able to provide the required capacity for the volume of traffic.

Other stretches of turnpike which visibly survive where they are not incorporated into modern surfaces can make for the engaging analysis of a landscape. Turnpike houses and tollhouses can also be spotted. Telford's A5 houses are usually octagonal; others can be recognised by the existence of a door or window (sometimes bricked up) bordering right on to the roadside. A worthwhile section of turnpike can be found west of Snowdon, south from Caernarfon on the neck of the Lleyn Peninsula.

On the east side of the A499, west of Glynllifon Country Park, the now redundant turnpike causeway can be seen as a very broad 'pavement' set back from the modern surface. Maen Llwyd standing stone indicates earlier passage in this landscape. South of the junction to Talysarn, the separation of the older route from the new becomes even more pronounced, with some of the turnpike route completely grassed over; a dense avenue of trees and the ruin of a turnpike house indicate the abandoned way. South of the turnpike house the former route is clear, eventually rejoining the flow of the A499 at Y Swan. The nearby Pont y Cim, with a date of 1612, is a charming seventeenth century bridge worth a closer look. Just to the east is another turnpike route with abandoned and adopted parts still visible. The modern monument on the roundabout which welcomes motorists entering from the A499 is a cromlech with a mining cart beneath it. These are two features iconic of North Wales' history and heritage: this is Penygroes and the Nantlle Valley.

Picking up the B4418 (Ffordd y Sir) to Talysarn, past Capel Curig one passes a most beautiful turnpike cottage every bit as attractive as the inappropriately-named Ty Hwll (the Ugly House). In keeping with the roofs of several properties in the town, the roof here is patterned with different shades of slate. The cottage is on the north side of the road. Observe the redundant road further on to the left-hand side (the north); one can begin extrapolating the flow of the former turnpike route, much of which before the cottage is now a footpath in front of a leisure centre.

Once this line or road is picked up its flow is clear for a couple miles as it heads towards Talysarn along Hyfrydle Road. Another lane to the north indicates even greater antiquity – Hen Lon or old lane. The old turnpike route is situated above and behind a wall that dominates the north side of the modern through-road. If one turns off the main road, it is possible to drive along the older route, albeit at a limited speed of 15 miles an hour. Traffic volume, road width, and today's personal ownership of vehicles is not something the Turnpike Trusts could have ever envisaged. This track becomes Station Road, and where the through-road can be rejoined at Bryncelyn Road there is a memorial to Talysarn's most famous resident, Robert Williams Parry, 1884–1956, remembered as "Bardd" or Bard.

Here the long terraces with cars parked out the front effectively turn the road a single-track lane now, to be driven along with care. Houses also rise up periodically upon outcrops, only to be dwarfed by the towering piles of upcast from the slate quarries which are mountainous against the houses. These are themselves dwarfed by Mynydd Tal-y-mignedd to the south and Mynydd Mawr to the north of the Nantlle Valley. The older route – still named Nantlle Road – stays to the north of the Afon Llyfni but is soon lost beneath the slate piles. There is a footpath alongside where the road would have been, but it is now impassable to vehicles. The route is picked up again at Nantlle where the B road rejoins its course at Glan Rhonwy. The modern route also passes one lake to its east and south (following the bend); Llyn Nantlle Uchaf was once paired with a lake to its west, Llyn Nantlle Isaf, but this was drained during operations relating to the slate works.

Iron Age remains dot the sides of the valley from beginning to end, from Caer Engan hillfort south of Penygroes, to numerous hut circles on the west side of Mynydd Mawr and east of Mynydd Drws y Coed. On the summits of the mountains, Bronze Age cairns testify to earlier passage through and above Dyffryn Nantlle.

The valley is named after Lleu, a native British God who frequented the valley and gave it his name, and who was reputed to hold his court at the nearby coastal fort of Dinas Dinlle. One may wonder if he had a part in the destruction of a chapel in 1892. Progressing through the valley on the left-hand side one comes across this chapel, which is still used on occasion and which has some clues in the dates high on its front. Just a little further on the right-hand side and nearer to the road there is a large boulder with a small plaque and memorial. This is a monument to the first church building that was constructed here in 1836, only to be destroyed by a rock which detached from Clogwyn y Barcut in 1892. The church was rebuilt further down the road, on the other side just next to the Afon Drws y Coed (the Gate or Door of the Wood); very soon the road will enter the Beddgelert Forest.

Opposite the chapel there are disused mine workers' houses; some nearer the road are still used, while there are others further back which are more skeletal in their remains and are evocative of industry having been and gone. King Edward I is reputed to have visited the valley himself to oversee some of the mine workings that were feeding his efforts against the Welsh.

Before the road finally ascends from the valley floor, the vista at the eastern end is possibly without equal in all of Snowdonia. Framed by the mountains either side, Snowdon is centre stage, flanked by Y Lliwedd and Moel Cynghorion with the dramatic craggy upthrust of Clogwyngarreg to the front. There are at least three milestones throughout the valley, with the last within the wall as the road angles to Llyn y Dwyarchen and then down to join the Caernarfon road (A4085) at Rhyd Ddu. Several old milestones and signposts also mark the route from Nantlle to Rhyd Ddu. A short distance north towards Caernarfon are the ruins of a tollhouse on the east of the road.

Southwards to Beddgelert the road remains a pleasant route, with several long straight stretches as it descends to the town of 'Gelert's Grave' though Nant Colwyn. A hillfort high above the curve of the A4085 to A498 watches the pass to the east in the direction of the fort Dinas Emrys, where archaeology, myth and history converge in rare agreement concerning links with Arthur and Vor-

Looking east – the A5 and A55 across Malltraeth Marsh; notice the undulations in the road surface, and the waterlogged area between the two roads.

tigern. To the west Moel Hebog presides, and to the south the Glaslyn river carves out the pass of the Aberglaslyn.

Another coach road, now completely bypassed by the modern route, lies a little east of Pont Aberglasyn. Between Nantmor and Croesor is the track that was once the main road to Dolgellau, descending onward via Maentwrog and Trawsfynydd. From the Glaslyn bridge a single track road eventually terminates in a steep unsurfaced way at Bwlchgwernog. It is understandable why this route swiftly fell out of favour in relation to a more circuitous but much smoother alternative. Hard turns, muddy ways alternating with uneven surfaces and some very steep stretches would have made a coach journey quite difficult. A crude stone bridge over the Afon Dylif would have been crossed with abject terror by any coaches descending from the ridge at speed. However, the slopes of Snowdon to the north, the archetypal mountain shape of Cnicht, and by striking contrast the rounded silhouette of Moelwyn Mawr, still make for a stunning journey through the terrain.

Redundant stretches of turnpike briefly divergent from the course of the A499 towards the Lleyn.

Left: Ruined turnpike house adjacent to the A499.

Left: Standing in the centre of the redundant flow of the turnpike road adjacent to the modern road and the turnpike house, left, at Penygroes.

Above: Mileposts between Drws y Coed and Rhyd Ddu.

Right: Looking north along the Glaslyn Pass at Pont Aberglaslyn pre1925; Postcard in author's collection, copyright holder and publisher not identifiable.

Left: Bridge over the Afon Dylif which carried the eighteenth century coach road from Aberglaslyn to Croesor; Cnicht Mountain to the rear.

Above: Looking west along the road to Drws y Coed and Nantlle.

ENDNOTES

The NPRN references in the Coflein citations are the unique numbers assigned to those entries in the Historic Environment Record; entering the NPRN in the relevant field on the database will take the user straight to the record concerned.

Preface

1. Rogers, B, 2003, 34.
2. See reports produced by Hopewell and by Silvester.
3. Godwin & Toulson.
4. Bryson, 248.

Chapter One – Overview of Roads and Trackways of North Wales

1. Lynch, 1995, 12.
2. www.pastscape.org.uk, Monument Types Thesaurus.
3. Borrow, 291.
4. Wilson, 300–301.
5. Waddelove, 5–6.
6. Moore-Colyer, 2002, 59.
7. Crofts, 16.
8. Bradley, 273–274.
9. Bonser, 227, 228.

Chapter Two – Prehistoric Trackways

1. Coflein, NPRN 93620.
2. Coflein, NPRN 406228.
3. Burnham, 1995, 22–23.
4. Gibson, 139.
5. Similar to the pairing of cairn circles at Moel Goedog: Cefn Caer Euni (SH993410) near Bala, with a later hillfort nearby, is a pairing formed by a cairn circle and a kerb circle across an ancient track. Further south to the south-west there is Coed y Bedo, a solitary standing stone at SH967400, believed to have been part of a track heading north-west from the Bala area over Foel Goch to Cerrigydrudion.
6. Burl, 189.
7. Burl, 192.
8. Hughes, 30.
9. 2007 saw an investigation into the exact location of this site, with more work to be carried out in May 2008 – see www.cpat.org.uk/projects/longer/

cwmmawr/cwmmawr.htm.

10. Brown, 73.

11. Longueville-Jones, 269; Brown, 71.

12. Brown, 73.

13. Brown, 79.

14. Cope, 323; additionally a conversation with a former colleague who is involved in lay ministry in the area yielded an unhesitating 'yes' when enquiring about this matter.

15. Knowles and Parkin, 32.

Chapter Three – Roman Roads

1. Silvester, 2003, 3.

2. See www.indigogroup.co.uk/edge/Boudica2.htm Bob Trubshaw, "Did Boudica die in Flintshire?"

3. Davies, F., 348. For further examples of discoveries from this period see also pages 24, 61, and 81.

4. Explore the route using Google Earth if internet access is available.

5. Longueville-Jones, 268.

6. Senior, 1991, 16–17.

7. Text from these milestones courtesy of displays at Bangor Museum.

8. Thorpe, 184.

9. Bromwich, 442.

10. Davies, F., 25.

11. Bromwich, 342.

12. The small scale Ordnance Survey map of Roman Britain appears to project a more direct course to the west of Mynydd Cribau, with no reference to the eastern segments given in the body of the text as an indirect route.

13. Silent black and white footage from the aftermath of the disaster in 1925 can be seen here www.gtj.org.uk/en/filmitems/29132.

14. Coflein, NPRN 404709.

15. Lynch, 1995, 94–96 gives a brief and helpful analysis of this site.

16. A route beyond the geographical limit of this work is from Wroxeter to Forden Gaer, with a possible route west from Shrewsbury following the line of the ridge south of Cardeston and Middletown. The route follows the B4386 though Yockleton and Stoney Stretton to Westbury, then arcs around through Vennington along the crest of Long Mountain, past Beacon Ring hillfort, descending to Forden and its strategic guarding of the Severn crossing.

Chapter Four – Roads and Trackways of Pilgrimage

1. Palmer and Palmer, 213.

2. Webb, 1.

3. John and Rees, 118; the exact date and numbers slaughtered at the Battle of Chester are given differently depending upon sources.

4. John & Rees, 54—55, evaluate reasons as to the apparent lack of Welsh ampullae and badges.

5. John & Rees, 56.

6. Coflein, NPRN 43901; the church at Llandanwg has a small display elaborating its case for a fifth century foundation of St Tanwg's.

7. Lynch, 126–128.

8. John and Rees, 156.

9. Coflein, NPRN 309579.

10. Ainsworth and Wilmott, 7–9.

11. Bradley, 1905, 349.

12. A fictional story based upon such superstition was written by a clergyman, Islwyn Ffowc Ellis: "Y Gromlech yn yr Haidd"– 'The Cromlech in the Barley Field', which records the unfortunate events which befall those who tamper with the tomb. Only available in Welsh, published by Gomer.

13. For extensive information, see www.british-history.ac.uk/report.aspx?compid=19191.

14. John and Rees, 67.

15. Personal correspondence and telephone calls with people in the area confirm that the well should be open to access by polite enquiry at the house adjoining it.

16. A number of accommodation huts are cited as existing in this field; has any archaeology had been done to confirm this, as at other places so named?

17. Coflein, NPRN 32224.

18. Coflein, NPRN 302295.

19. John and Rees, 153.

20. Coflein, NPRN 43815, 32200.

21. Coflein, NPRIN 32205, NPRN 43766.

22. Coflein, NPRN 11557.

23. Coflein, NPRN 95287.

24. Coflein, NPRN 32220.

25. Coflein, NPRN 43707; the possible anachronism here is recognised, and is due to uncertain dating in respective parts of the building.

26. Coflein, NPRN 32208; Davies, 34, describes a similar arrangement at Llanengan – but as there is only one well recorded there; it must be this arrangement of which he speaks. Further confusion is raised y the fact that modern map incorrectly records the name, which should be Ffynnon Dduw.

27. Coflein, NPRN 301084.

28. Jones, 34.

29. Coflein, NPRN 32189.

30. John and Rees, 157.

31. Coflein, NPRN 43798.

32. Coflein, NPRN 32219.

33. The claim for this being the number of the saints buried on Bardsey is on a National Trust Tourist Information sign at Braich y Pwll.

34. Burnham, 179.

35. Barnwell, 1873.

36. Investigation of the monuments record yields no current entry for this; is it now lost?

37. Some sources say granddaughter.

38. Coflein, NPRN 43868, NRPN 32374.

39. Coflein, NPRN 43865, NPRN 401210.

40. See John and Rees, Chapter 13 for further information on the route.

Chapter Five – Drove Roads and Trackways

1. Borrow, 184.

2. Bradley, 100.

3. Borrow, 183.

4. Ibid.

5. Ibid., 291.

6. Toulson, 1980, 20.

7. Moore-Colyer, 2002, has treated the drove routes of South and Mid-Wales with admirable detail, while Godwin and Toulson in their book combine a commendable walking guide with drove routes although this makes tracing the droveways very confusing in places.

8. Moore-Colyer, 2002, 78.

9. When visiting with a friend, a fortuitous conversation with a neighbour pulling out from their drive yielded the verbal information that it was commonly held to be a stone placed there within the last 300 years at the most, as a family memorial to a beloved mother.

10. Dutton, 8.

11. Coflein, NPRN 282001.

12. Coflein, NPRN 282016.

13. Colfein, NPRN 282005.

14. Bonser, 192–193.

15. Coflein, NPRN 269091.

16. Toulson proposes another route which would bypass some of the toll charges north of Dollgellau and would instead head across country to Llanfachreth. However, tracing this route on maps leaves the droveway in the wilderness with no obvious indication of how to make headway to Bala. A blanket 'on to Bala' is given, and the terrain on the map gives no straightforward way on.

17. Bradley, 432.

18. Moore-Colyer, 2002, 82. For an unsurpassable account of this route in the turnpike era, see Moore-Colyer, 1984.

19. Bonser, 186–187.

20. Bradley, 3.

21. Bradley, 7.

22. Bonser, 186–187.

23. Reported to me at the Oswestry and Borders History and Archaeology Group was the fact that three Scots Pine signified a drove route.

24. Display at Oriel Ynys Mon, Llangefni, Anglesey.

25. Moore-Colyer, 2002, 78.

26. A. Aikin, "Journal of a Tour through North Wales and Part of Shropshire", 1797, page 153; cited in Bonser, 47.

27. Bradley, 248.

28. Bradley, 223.

29. Knowles and Parkin, 38.

Chapter Six – Development of Roads and Trackways to Turnpikes and Telford

1. Crofts, 17.

2. Trinder et al, 10.

3. Knowles and Parkin, 32.

4. Bradley, 125.

5. Crofts, 12–13.

6. Dutton, 30. Like many books on old roads, sources are not cited, limited or no bibliographies are given, and the profusion of interesting features which make a rewarding walk but which are not a part of the ancient route, all serve to make tracing the actual line of the track difficult, hindering deeper interpretation and others wishing to follow research from where the earlier writers left off.

7. Coflein, NPRN 23804.

8. Coflein, NPRN, 23501.

9. Cited on displays at Oriel Ynys Mon, Llangefni, Anglesey.

10. Coflein, NPRN 27441.

11. Thorpe, 192.

12. Bradley, 268.

13. Trinder et al, 12.

14. Bartlett, 126.

15. Stuart, 436, 437.

16. Rolt, 140.

17. Cope, 145.

18. Coflein, NPRN 23839.

19. Colt, 144.

20. Stuart, 442–443.

21. Quartermaine et al, 92.

22. Holy Bible, New International Version.

23. Rogers, B., 144.

BIBLIOGRAPHY

This bibliography represents works referred to in the text, consulted during research and of potential use to the reader wishing to research the subject even further. Related websites are given at the end of each section.

Multi-Period and General

Aris, M. "*Historic Landscapes of the Great Orme*", Gwasg Carreg Gwalch, Llanrwst (1996).

Arnold, C.J., and Davies, J.L. "*Roman and Early Mediaeval Wales*", Sutton Publishing, Thrupp (2000).

Bagley, J.J. , Cheshire Community Council, Chester, (1972).

Bartlett, W.B. "*The Taming of the Dragon*", Sutton Publishing, Thrupp (2003).

Bick, D. "*The Old Metal Mines of Mid-Wales – parts 4 and 5 – West Montgomeryshire, Aberdovey, Dinas Mawddy and Llangynog*", The Pound House, Newent (1990).

Bingley, W. "*North Wales: Delineated from two excursions through all the interesting parts of that highly beautiful and romantic country and intended as a guide to future tourists*", first published 1814, Cedric Chivers Ltd, Bristol (1998).

Borrow, G. "*Wild Wales*", Collins, London & Glasgow (1862).

Bradley, A.G. "*Highways and Byways in North Wales*", Macmillan and Co., London (1905).

Breese, G. "*The Bridges of Wales*", Gwasg Carreg Gwalch, Llanrwst (2001).

Bromwich, R. "*Trioedd Ynys Prydein*", University of Wales Press, Cardiff (2006).

Brown, I. "*Discovering a Welsh Landscape – Archaeology in the Clwydian Range*", Windgather Press, Bollington (2004).

Bryson, B. "*Notes from a Small Island*", Black Swan, London, (1996).

Bullock, J.D. "*A History of Cheshire Volume III: Pre-Conquest Cheshire 383—1066*" (General Editor).

Burnham, H. "*A Guide to Ancient and Historic Wales – Clwyd and Powys*", HMSO, London (1995).

Davies, E. "*The Prehistoric and Roman Remains of Flintshire*", (Pages Missing).

Dutton, R. J. A. "*Hidden Highways of North Wales*", Redwood Books, Trowbridge (2003).

Ellis, B. "*The History of Halkyn Mountain*", Helygain, Halkyn (1998).

Gregory, D. "*Country Churchyards in Wales*", Gwasg Carreg Gwalch, Llanrwst (1991).

Gregory, D. "*Wales after 1536*", Gwasg Carreg Gwalch, Llanrwst (1995).

Hainsworth, J. "*Llangynog: A Village Trail*", St Melangell Centre, Pennant Melangell (2006).

Harris, R. "*Walks in Ancient Wales*", Sigma Leisure, Wilmslow (2003).

Hughes, W. "*Anglesey Past & Present*", Gwasg Carreg Gwalch, Llanrwst (1999).

Jenner, L. "*Walking in the Vale of Clwyd and the Denbigh Moors*", Mara Publications, Helsby (2000).

Jervoise, E. "*The Ancient Bridges of Wales and Western England*", The Architectural Press, London (1936).

Knowles, D.S., and Parkin, B.E. "*Just One Parish – The History of Llanarmon yn Ial*", self published and first printed to commemorate the Golden Jubilee of the Llanarmon yn Ial Women's Institute in 1973, reprinted for Llanarmon and District Conservation Society (2003).

Lynch, F. "*A Guide to Ancient and Historic Wales – Gwynedd*", HMSO, London (1995).

Main, L. "*The Spirit Paths of Wales*", Cicerone Press, Milnthorpe (2000).

Morgan, P. "*Wales An Illustrated History*", Tempus Publishing Limited, Stroud (2005).

Moore-Colyer, R. "*Roads and Trackways of Wales*", Moorland Publishing Ltd, Ashbourne (1984).

Morris, J. General Editor, "*Domesday Book: A Survey of the Counties Of England Compiled by the direction of King William I Winchester 1086*", Morgan, P., editor "Cheshire: Including Lancashire, Cumbria and North Wales", Phillimore, Chichester (1978).

Musson, C. "*Wales from the Air: Patterns of Past and Present*", Royal Commission on the Ancient & Historical Monuments of Wales, (1994).

Richards, R. "*Two Bridges over Menai*", Gwasg Carreg Gwalch, Llanrwst (2004).

Rogers, B. "*The Bank Manager and the Holy Grail: Travels to the Wilder Reaches of Wales*", Aurum Press Ltd, London (2003).

Rogers, C. "*Walking on the Lleyn Peninsula*", Mara Publications, Helsby (1999).

Senior, M. "*The Crossing of the Conwy*", Gwasg Carreg Gwalch, Llanrwst (1991).

Senior, M. "*North Wales in the Making*", Gwasg Carreg Gwalch, Llanrwst (2003).

Stuart, R. "*Cyclopedia of architecture, historical, descriptive, typographical, decorative, theoretical and mechanical, alphabetically arranged, familiarly explained, and adapted to the comprehension of workmen, etc., etc.*", A S Banres & Co (1854). Available online through GoogleBooks.

Thorpe, L., trans. "*Gerald of Wales – The Journey through Wales / The Description of Wales*", Penguin Books Ltd, Harmondsworth (1978).

Tucker, N. "*North Wales in the Civil War*", Gee, Denbigh, (1958). (Details uncertain due to missing pages.)

Wright, K.A. "*Gentle are its Songs*", Sir Gerald Nabarro (Publications) Ltd, Birmingham (1973).

"*The Cambrian Journal Volume I*", The Cambrian Institute, London (1854). Available online through Google Books.

Archaeology Data Service/Arts and Humanities Data Service: ads.ahds.ac.uk/catalogue/search/index.cfm

BRITARCH discussion list: www.britarch.ac.uk

British History Online: www.british-history.ac.uk

Clwyd Powys Archaeological Trust: www.cpat.org.uk

COFLEIN: www.coflein.gov.uk

Countryside Council for Wales: www.ccw.gov.uk

Gathering the Jewels – The Website for Welsh Cultural History: www.gtj.org.uk

Google Books: books.google.com

Gwynedd Archaeological Trust: www.heneb.co.uk

The Megalithic Portal (Prehistory, Ancient Crosses and Holy Wells): www.megalithic.info

Northern Earth – Journeys in Living Landscapes: www.northernearth.co.uk

Pastscape: www.pastscape.org.uk

Robinson, M. M. "*Abandoned Landscapes – A series of walks in North Wales*", published online only at www.megalithic.co.uk/article.php?sid=2146412525

Royal Commission on the Ancient and Historical Monuments of Wales: www.rcahmw.gov.uk

Prehistoric

Barber, C, and Williams, G.W. "*The Ancient Stones of Wales*", Blorenge Books, Abergavenny (1989).

Burl, A. "*The Stone Circles of Britain, Ireland, and Brittany*", Yale University Press, New Haven and London (2000).

Burrow, S. "*The Tomb Builders: In Wales 4000 – 3000BC*", National Museum Wales Books, Cardiff (2006).

Cope, J. "*The Modern Antiquarian*", Thorsons, London, 1998.

Gibson, A. "*Cursus Monuments and Possible Cursus Monuments in Wales: avenues for research (or roads to nowhere?)*", published in "*Pathways and Ceremonies: The Cursus Monuments of Britain and Ireland*", Barclay, A., and Harding, J., Oxbow Books, Oxford (1999).

Green, S. "*Ice Age Hunters: Neanderthals and Early Modern Hunters in Wales*", National Museums and Galleries of Wales, Cardiff (1991).

Longueville-Jones, H. "*Early British Remains in Wales*", Archaeologica Cambrensis, 1885, 262–270

Lynch, F., Aldhouse-Green, S., and Davies, J.L. "*Prehistoric Wales*", Sutton Publishing, Thrupp (2000).

McCormack, B. "*Prehistoric Sites of Montgomeryshire*", Logaston Press, Little Logaston (2006).

Morgan, V & P. "*Prehistoric Cheshire*", Landmark Publishing Ltd, Ashbourne (2004).

Nash, G. "*The Architecture of Death – Neolithic Chambered Tombs in Wales*", Logaston Press, Little Logaston (2006).

Senior, M. "*Hillforts of Northern Wales*", Gwasg Garreg Gwalch, Llanrwst (2005).

Heather & Hillforts – The Clwydian Range: www.heatherandhillforts.co.uk

The Modern Antiquarian: www.themodernantiquarian.com

Roman

Ainsworth, S. & T. Wilmott. "*Chester Amphitheatre*", Chester City Council and English Heritage (2005).

Cantrell, J. & A. Rylance. "*Sarn Helen*", Cicerone Press, Milnthorpe (1992).

Davies, J.L., and Jones, R.H. "*Roman Camps in Wales and The Marches*", University of Wales Press, Cardiff (2006).

Hopewell, D. "*Roman Roads in North-West Wales (Revision 4)*", unpublished Gwynedd Archaeological Trust Report 668 (project G1632) (2007).

Hopewell, D. "*Roman Fort Environs 2002/2003*", unpublished Gwynedd Archaeological Trust Report 479 (project G1632) (2003).

Mason, D.J.P. "*Roman Chester – City of the Eagles*", Tempus Publishing Ltd, Stroud (2001).

Silvester, R.J. "*The Clwyd Powys Archaeological Trust The Roman Roads of East and North-East Wales – The First Report*", CPAT Report No. 527, Welshpool (2003).

Silvester, R.J. "*The Clwyd Powys Archaeological Trust The Roman Roads of East and North-East Wales – A Second Report*", CPAT Report No. 621, Welshpool (2004).

Wacher, J. "*Roman Britain*", Sutton Publishing Ltd, Thrupp (2001).

Waddelove, E. "*The Roman Roads of North Wales – Recent Discoveries*", privately published, Ruthin (1999).

Wilson, R.J.A. "*A Guide to the Roman Remains in Britain*", Constable & Robinson Ltd, London (2002).

Roman Britain: www.roman-britain.org

Pilgrimage

Barnwell, E.L. "*The Nevern Rock-Cross*", Archaeologica Cambrensis 28 (1873) 370–373.

Bord, J. "*Cures and Curses*", Heart of Albion Press, Loughborough (2006).

Bord, J. "*Holy Wells in Britain: a guide*", Heart of Albion Press, Loughborough (2008).

Chadwick, H. "*The Early Church*", Penguin, London (1990).

Davis, P. "*Sacred Springs – In Search of the Holy Wells and Spas of Wales*", Blorenge Books, Abergavenny (2003).

Edwards, G.W. "*A Short History of the Churches and Neighbourhood of Llanbadrig, Llanfechell, Llanfflewin and Bodewyrd*". No publishing data included in booklet.

Green, J. "*Holy Ways of Wales*", Y Lolfa, Talybont (2000).

John, T and Rees, M. "*Pilgrimage: A Welsh Perspective*", Gomer Press, Llandysul (2002).

Jones, A. "*Every Pilgrim's Guide to Celtic Britain and Ireland*", The Canterbury Press, Norwich (2002).

Peck, C. "*Between Earth and Heaven: A Journey into Sacred Space*", Arthur James, Berkhamsted (1997).

Peck, M. S. "*In Search of Stones: A Pilgrimage of Faith, Reason and Discovery*", Simon & Schuster, London (1997).

Webb, D. "*Pilgrimage in Medieval England*", Hambledon and London, London and New York (2000).

"*Corpus Christi Tremeirchion*", Tremerchion Parochial Church Council (2006).

The Cistercian Way: cistercian-way.newport.ac.uk

The National Wells Index: nationalwellsindex.org.uk

St Hywyn's Church: www.st-hywyn.org.uk

Drovers and Packhorses

Bonser, K.J. "*The Drovers*", Macmillan & Co., London and Basingstoke (1970).

Crofts, J. "*Packhorse Waggon and Post*", Routledge and Kegan Paul Limited, London (1967).

Godwin, F. and Toulson, S. "*The Drovers' Roads of Wales*", Wildwood House Ltd, London (1978).

Moore-Colyer, R. "*Welsh Cattle Drovers*", Landmark Publishing Ltd, Ashbourne (2002).

Toulson, S. "*The Drovers*", Shire Publications Ltd, (1980).

Telford, Turnpikes and Today

Reader, W.J. "*Macadam – The McAdam Family and the Turnpike Roads 1798—1861*", William Heinemann Ltd, London (1980).

Rolt, L.T.C. "*Thomas Telford*", Sutton Publishing Ltd, Thrupp (2007).

Trinder, B., Turner, R., and Quartermaine, J. "*Thomas Telford's Holyhead Road: The A5 in North Wales*", Council for British Archaeology, (2002).

Wright, G.N. "*Turnpike Roads*", Shire Publications Ltd, (1992).

The Motorway Archive: www.iht.org/motorway/a55wales

Traffic Wales: www.traffic-wales.com

INDEX